RAND NATIONAL DEFENSE RESEARCH INSTITUTE

Transformation of Taiwan's Reserve Force

Ian Easton, Mark Stokes, Cortez A. Cooper, Arthur Chan

Prepared for the Office of the Under Secretary of Defense

Approved for public release; distribution unlimited

For more information on this publication, visit www.rand.org/t/RR1757

Library of Congress Cataloging-in-Publication Data is available for this publication.
ISBN: 978-0-8330-9706-4

Cover: Photo by REUTERS/Patrick Lin.

Support RAND
Make a tax-deductible charitable contribution at
www.rand.org/giving/contribute

www.rand.org

Preface

This report provides an overview of Taiwan's reserve force structure and describes its roles, missions, capabilities, and challenges. The authors also provide strategic-level analysis and make recommendations for future Taiwan reserve force roles, missions, and capabilities, based on the requirement to counter People's Republic of China advantages in air and maritime power-projection capabilities. Finally, they also identify potential enabling capabilities and specialist units that Taiwan could incorporate into the reserve force structure and examine several case studies of reserve forces in other countries to identify examples germane to Taiwan's situation.

This research was sponsored by the Office of the Under Secretary of Defense for Policy and conducted within the Forces and Resources Policy Center (FRP) of the RAND National Defense Research Institute, a federally funded research and development center sponsored by the Office of the Secretary of Defense, the Joint Staff, the Unified Combatant Commands, the Navy, the Marine Corps, the defense agencies, and the Defense Intelligence Community.

For more information on the Forces and Resources Policy Center, see www.rand.org/nsrd/ndri/centers/frp or contact the director (contact information is provided on the web page).

Contents

Summary

Despite the growth in trade and investment between Taiwan and the People's Republic of China (PRC) over the past two decades, and relative stability in the overall relationship since 2008, prospects for the two governments resolving their political differences regarding sovereignty over Taiwan appear slim in the foreseeable future. From Beijing's perspective, Taiwan and its democratic system of government pose an existential challenge to PRC authority.[1] The PRC has long sought the political subordination of Taiwan under its "One China" principle, but people on Taiwan increasingly identify themselves as citizens of a state that is separate and distinct from the PRC. As a result, the Chinese Communist Party considers the capacity for use of force, including the invasion and occupation of Taiwan, to be the most important strategic mission of the People's Liberation Army (PLA).

Taiwan has relied on various material and intangible factors to deter PRC use of force and other forms of coercion, including shortcomings in the PLA's ability to project power significantly across the Taiwan Strait, technological advantages of Taiwan's armed forces, and geographic characteristics of the Taiwan Strait. Many of these advantages, however, are eroding over time.

Taiwan is taking important steps to deter PRC use of force and to defend itself should deterrence fail. Taiwan's armed forces are improving their war reserve stocks, investing in a defense industrial base, advancing their ability to carry out joint operations, and

---

[1] By "existential," we mean that the Chinese Communist Party leadership of the PRC considers eventual unification of Taiwan under its "One Country, Two Systems" principle a "core interest" of the PRC, and Taiwan independence a threat to party rule.

strengthening their personnel system. In the area of personnel, fiscal limitations and a reduced force structure, alongside growing personnel costs and increased PLA military capabilities, highlight the need for more-innovative approaches to personnel management. To create a more streamlined military, Taiwan is transitioning to an all-volunteer force and reducing its active-duty force from 275,000 to approximately 175,000 personnel.

One area in which Taiwan could increase investments to enhance its military capabilities against the Chinese threat is the reserve force. Taiwan's defense establishment maintains a significant reserve force that can mobilize to augment active-duty personnel. In this report, we provide an overview of how Taiwan's reserve force is structured and describe its roles, missions, capabilities, and challenges. We also analyze the Taiwan reserve force's role in cross-Strait competition and make recommendations for future Taiwan reserve force roles, missions, and capabilities, based on the requirement to counter PRC advantages in air and maritime power-projection capabilities.

If Taiwan's leaders expect the reserve force to mobilize to face an increasingly capable threat from the Chinese mainland, particularly as Taiwan's active force reduces in numbers and transitions to a volunteer force, it is essential that Taipei reconceptualize its reserve force. To offset growing PLA advantages, the current strategic reserve will need to develop a new reserve concept—potentially involving changes to reserve force size, structure, roles, missions, equipment, and training. With this in mind, what are the most promising areas in which to invest in reserve force modernization and transformation? The Office of the Under Secretary of Defense for Policy asked RAND to explore and assess the following areas:

- **Task 1. Assess current Taiwan reserve force structure, roles, and missions.** Based on publicly available research and expert discussions, assess current Taiwan reserve force structure, roles, and missions. Identify potential gaps in capabilities to meet future threats.
- **Task 2. Analyze needed future capabilities.** Conduct a strategic-level analysis and make recommendations for Taiwan's

future reserve force, based on the requirement to counter PRC advantages in air and maritime power-projection capabilities.

- **Task 3. Identify needed enablers.** Identify potential enabling capabilities and specialist units that Taiwan could incorporate into the reserve force structure.
- **Task 4. Summary and final recommendations.** Recommend reserve force transitional needs in the context of Taiwan's broader future force requirements.

We based this study on a comprehensive literature review and discussions with defense experts in Taiwan and the United States in the latter half of 2015. The research includes an appendix providing a brief comparative analysis of reserve force transformation in other countries, to glean lessons potentially relevant to Taiwan reserve force reform.

Reserve Force Roles, Missions, and Capabilities

Taiwan's Armed Forces Reserve Command has both peacetime and wartime missions. In peacetime, the command is responsible for managing the tri-service reserve system; organizing and training reserve units; recruiting new talent; and preparing, certifying, and executing mobilization plans. Of the Reserve Command's peacetime missions, preparing and certifying mobilization plans is the highest priority. The PRC's military is close to Taiwan's territory and equipped with ballistic missiles and other weapons intended to minimize warning time. Taiwan therefore must maintain the capacity to mobilize its reserve force rapidly and under stressful conditions.

The Reserve Command is further responsible for planning, inspecting, assessing, and certifying Taiwan's national capacity to mobilize defense assets. Mobilization in the Taiwan context entails more than just bringing latent military capabilities into action. Mobilization is an all-out national defense effort that affects the entire population. This includes the planned integration of civil defense units and civilian contractor assets into military operations for homeland defense. It also includes preparing for the mobilization of defense industrial facilities, critical infrastructure, and relevant civilian defense companies. Additionally, in wartime, the Reserve Command is responsible for providing mobilized reserve brigades to operational commanders.

Taiwan's leadership places an extraordinarily high priority on mobilization. For example, Taiwan has not reduced its mobilization budget, in spite of the otherwise across-the-board cuts undertaken by the Taiwan military as part of its force transformation. Military units involved in certifying and executing mobilization plans have been spared from cuts, and some reserve brigades have seen their budgets increase, albeit modestly. Our analysis, however, suggests that Taiwan's Reserve Command does not have the needed budgetary resources to emphasize frequent and realistic training to maintain reservist skill sets. Moreover, new conscripts going into the reserve force may not have received sufficiently rigorous training, due to new, abbreviated training rotation schemes. More reserve training likely will be necessary to meet Taiwan's envisioned defense planning requirements.

Taiwan's reserve force capabilities appear to be keeping pace with many, but not all, aspects of the changing threat environment. On the positive side of the ledger, Taiwan has demonstrated an outstanding ability to mobilize its military and society to respond to both man-made and natural disasters. However, the PLA is rapidly modernizing, with the objective of being able to project overwhelming force across the Taiwan Strait. As the number of Taiwan's active-duty soldiers, sailors, airmen, and marines continue to decline, reservists will need to assume increasingly difficult missions. Taiwan's current approach to reserve force training may be appropriate for many noncombat support personnel in the system, but it seems inadequate for maintaining the readiness of those reserve units that would see combat in the event of an all-out Chinese invasion.

Prospects for an Enhanced Strategic Role

With its large size, scope of mission, and range of capabilities, Taiwan's reserve force represents a significant strategic means for achieving Taipei's objective to deter PRC use of force against the island. As the political-military challenge from the PRC grows in the years ahead, the reserve force may need to play a more prominent role in Taipei's strategic competition with Beijing. Our analysis suggests that by linking reserve force reform and modernization efforts with leadership statements, military exercises, arms sales, and other politically sensitive aspects of Taiwan's defense, Taipei can confront authorities in Beijing with the reality that any invasion campaign they may consider undertaking would meet with overwhelming resistance. This would be a new role for the reserve force, and one for which it appears well suited.

To position itself more effectively for a long-term strategic competition, Taiwan should also consider future reserve force roles, missions, and capabilities to counter PRC capability advantages in projecting an invasion force across, over, above, and through specific geographic battle spaces. We assess that this requires bolstering reserve force capabilities to deny the PLA unimpeded access to the information (electromagnetic), air, and maritime domains. There are significant constraints to PLA amphibious operations inherent to the unique military geography of the Taiwan Strait area. Taiwan could potentially better exploit these with a future mix of reserve force investments targeted to specific PLA vulnerabilities. Our concluding recommendations fall into three categories:

1.   Employ the reserve force as an instrument of statecraft for deterring PRC use of force and other forms of coercion. New initiatives along this line of effort might include the following:
     – Publicly highlight the reserve force in leadership statements, published defense strategy documents, and the Taiwan press. As an example, recent reporting notes moves to correct administrative shortcomings in call-up training.[2]
     – Highlight the reserve force at Taiwan's annual HAN KUANG exercises. Mobilizing multiple reserve brigades during the annual HAN KUANG exercises and integrating them into

---

[2] Joseph Yeh, "Defense Ministry Amends Reservist Call-Up Loophole," *China Post*, April 22, 2016.

live-fire events with active-duty units likely would be an effective initiative in this regard.

- Engage in military-to-military exchanges with the U.S. Department of Defense, including the Office of the Secretary of Defense, the Joint Staff, and the U.S. Army, that directly relate to improving the reserve force. Considerations could include establishment of a joint reserve force working group, led on the U.S. side by the Office of the Assistant Secretary of Defense for Manpower and Reserve Affairs, regular visits to the United States by senior leaders of Taiwan's Reserve Command, and professional military education and technical training in the United States for Taiwan reservists.

- Organize the reserves in keeping with plans for the era of the all-volunteer force. As part of the transition to a more strategically focused reserve force, Taiwan authorities should consider a role for the reserves in providing technically specialized personnel and units to augment the active force. Reserve augmentation of pilots and information technology specialists, for example, would send a clear signal to Beijing that the Taiwan reserves would add considerable capability in mission critical areas.

2. Consider how the reserve force can undermine PRC advantages in the initial stages of an invasion scenario and better exploit domain-specific and geographic aspects of the conflict. New concepts along this line might include the following:

- Exploring how the reserve force can contribute more during phase one and phase two operations (force preservation and joint combat) so that Taiwan does not cede the strategic initiative to the PRC at the outset of conflict.

- Considering where the reserve force can better exploit the favorable geography of the Taiwan Strait battlespace to target critical PLA vulnerabilities in projecting power.

3. Develop future reserve roles, missions, and capabilities, including specialist units and specialist jobs to incorporate into the reserve force structure, to exploit enabling capabilities, and pro-

vide additional equipment and training resources to support these units. Three particularly promising areas are:

– Constraining access to the electromagnetic domain by forming special reserve units composed of information and communication technology (ICT) experts for electronic and cyber warfare.
– Denying unimpeded access to the air domain by forming special reserve units for maintaining and operating large numbers of air defense missiles.
– Impeding access to the sea domain by forming special reserve units for operations employing antiship missiles, expanded mine warfare capabilities, advanced antisubmarine warfare technologies, and unmanned surveillance systems.

To reinforce and realize the advantages from the recommendations above, Taiwan must develop and resource new training programs. Current reserve force training is insufficient to meet the challenges posed by the increasing threat from the PLA. To be effective, the units and personnel focused on the new areas we recommend must be indistinguishable from their counterparts in the regular force, allowing them to bring their special skills to bear quickly during wartime operations. It is imperative that specialist reservists spend significant quantities of time (at least two or three weeks) every year engaged in intense and realistic training. This requires the government of Taiwan to increase funding allotted for training, education, and personnel development.

Constraints on Taiwan's defense budget and competition for resources are pushing Taipei to consider more innovative employment of its military force to meet the growing threat from mainland China. One area of interest, explored in this study, is how Taiwan can use reserve forces more effectively against the growing number of challenges posed to Taiwan by the PLA. Based on our analysis, there are many opportunities for reserve forces to play a significant role in undermining potential PRC military force projection capabilities, and in deterring use of force by becoming more conspicuously capable in specific domains and mission areas. We offer recommendations specifying what we believe to be the most promising areas in this regard and point to areas where further study and analysis could lead to enhanced Taiwan reserve force readiness and effectiveness.

Acknowledgments

The authors would like to thank Bernard Rostker, Kristen Gunness, and Randy Schriver for the insights and thoughtful recommendations proffered in the production of this report. The report benefited tremendously from their deep knowledge across the range of issues associated with reserve force reforms generally, and reserve force contributions to Taiwan's defense specifically. Their careful, constructive critiques and inputs were instrumental in moving this study through all the phases of our research, analysis, and final publication.

CHAPTER ONE

Introduction

Disagreement regarding the sovereign status of the island of Taiwan (or Republic of China [ROC]) has been a significant source of instability in the Asia-Pacific region since 1949, when Chiang Kai-shek and his Chinese Nationalist government fled to the island and Mao Zedong and his communist cohort established the People's Republic of China (PRC) on the Chinese mainland.[1] Despite the growth in cross-Taiwan Strait trade and investment over the past two decades, prospects for the two governments resolving political differences appear slim in the near future. From Beijing's perspective, Taiwan and its democratic system of government pose an existential challenge to the PRC and to the legitimacy of the Chinese Communist Party (CCP). The PRC has long sought the political subordination of Taiwan under its "One China" principle, viewing Taiwan as a renegade province awaiting unification, by force if necessary. People on Taiwan increasingly identify themselves as citizens of a state that is separate and distinct from the PRC.[2] As a result, the CCP considers the capacity for use of force, including the

---

[1] December 8, 1949, is the date that Chiang Kai-shek and his advisors officially moved the Republic of China government from the Chinese mainland to Taiwan. Bruce A. Elleman, *High Seas Buffer: The Taiwan Patrol Force, 1950–1979*, Newport, R.I.: Naval War College Press, 2012, p. 10.

[2] See, for example, Tseng Wei-chen and Chen Wei-han, "Unification Support Dives: Poll," *Taipei Times*, July 26, 2015; Ian Bremmer, "5 Statistics That Explained the World This Week," *Politico*, March 2, 2014; and Yuan-kang Wang, "Taiwan Public Opinion on Cross-Strait Security Issues: Implications for US Foreign Policy," *Strategic Studies Quarterly*, Summer 2013, p. 100.

invasion and occupation of Taiwan, to be the most important strategic mission of the People's Liberation Army (PLA).[3]

Over the past ten years, China has spoken of its most consequential security needs in terms of the protection or defense of its "core interests." Chinese leaders employ various formulations to describe core national interests. However, the most commonly encountered list consists of the following broad groupings:

- *Security*: Preserving China's basic political system and national security
- *Sovereignty*: Protecting national sovereignty, territorial integrity, and national unity
- *Development*: Maintaining international conditions for China's economic development.

The first core interest concerns the maintenance of China's basic political system, or CCP rule over the country. The credibility and viability of CCP control over the reins of power rests predominantly on the party's ability to sustain economic growth and defend national sovereignty. Accordingly, the second core interest concerns national sovereignty, territorial integrity, and national unity. PRC strategists view Taiwan, Xinjiang, and Tibet as areas of particular concern and sensitivity. The third category concerns those economic and other interests deemed vital to ensuring the sustained growth of the Chinese economy. This refers to the economic raw materials, markets, sea lines of communication, and other resources critical to sustaining the nation's development.

Chinese authorities have linked these core interests to eventual unification of Taiwan under PRC authority, and have raised expectations among China's citizenry that unification is a central component of China's reemergence as a great power. While there is no apparent timeline under which PRC leaders feel compelled to realize unifica-

---

[3] See U.S. Department of Defense, *Annual Report to Congress: Military and Security Developments Involving the People's Republic of China*, Washington, D.C., 2015. Also see Shou Xiaosong, ed., *Science of Military Strategy* [战略学], Beijing: Military Science Press, 2013, pp. 198–200.

tion, and peaceful efforts to achieve political objectives via economic and cultural integration with Taiwan remain Beijing's preferred course, tensions between the mainland and Taiwan are never far below the surface. No PRC leader can afford to be seen as weak on Taiwan, and China's ongoing military modernization efforts likely will give CCP leaders by 2020 a range of credible options to underpin Beijing's political goals. Use of military options to compel unification likely would be a last resort, founded on a perception by Beijing that some event or confluence of events was tantamount to Taiwan's permanent separation; but once military operations were under way, the risks of failing to achieve minimum political objectives through such operations would constrain the PRC's options for de-escalation. The survival of the CCP would be uncertain, and PLA plans and operations most likely reflect that reality.

The PLA is developing capabilities not only to deter and/or prevent Taiwan from formally declaring or otherwise establishing independence, but also to deter, delay, deny, and defeat third-party intervention (mainly by U.S. forces) in a cross-Strait crisis or conflict. Counter-intervention capabilities and investments have been a priority for the PLA since the 1990s, although, as China's overseas presence expands, the PLA has also increasingly focused on security interests in other areas in the region and across the globe.

In the event Taiwan attempts to become independent or PRC leadership decides to try to force unification, the PLA has numerous campaigns that it could conduct against Taiwan and any involved U.S. forces. These include a conventional joint fire strike campaign, a joint blockade campaign to sever Taiwan's economic and informational connections, a joint island-landing campaign to seize and occupy the island, and an anti–air raid campaign that includes defeating air raids through strikes on an adversary's air bases and aircraft carriers. In a comprehensive operation to compel Taiwan unification with the mainland in the 2020 period, all of these campaigns and other supporting efforts likely would feature in the PLA plan. China could also have a nuclear counter-strike campaign at the ready, to maintain and signal a credible nuclear deterrent during such a conflict. The PRC maintains a declaratory policy of no first use of nuclear weapons. However, there are ambiguities regarding the point at which China would determine that adversary strikes against Chinese targets had crossed a strategic threshold warranting nuclear response.

As a result, Taiwan faces perhaps the most stressful set of security challenges in the world today. Over the past decades, Taiwan has relied on various material and intangible factors to deter PRC use of force and other forms of coercion, including shortcomings in the PLA's ability to project power across the Taiwan Strait, technological advantages of Taiwan's armed forces, and geographic characteristics of the Taiwan Strait. Many of these advantages, however, are eroding over time.

Taiwan military planners do not openly delineate the assumptions that drive force development decisions in this challenging environment. Two assumptions, however, appear to be central to force development activities across the board. First, in the absence of a formal U.S. alliance commitment, Taiwan military planners must assume an independent defense, while preparing for the possibility of U.S. intervention. The concept of independent defense—the need to prepare for a contingency in which outside assistance was uncertain—has its roots in former Chief of Staff Hau Pei-tsun's strategy articulated after the abrogation of the U.S.-ROC Mutual Defense Treaty in 1979. Although the subject of some debate, this assumption appears to remain at the core of Taiwan planning and reinforces the need for a large reserve force that can efficiently mobilize and support operations to prevent a *fait accompli* by an increasingly capable PLA.[4]

Second, Taiwan planners expect that they will have about four weeks of warning that the PRC is preparing to launch an invasion of Taiwan. These planners recognize that the PLA could conduct certain punitive military strikes with little or no warning, but an invasion aimed at compelling unification would require significant PRC mobilization activity and thereby provide an opportunity for Taiwan to mobilize reserve forces to meet the threat.

---

4 "Don't Expect US Military Aid: General," *Taipei Times*, February 8, 2006; "MND Estimates China's Future Military Stance," *China Post*, February 8, 2006; Kang Shih-jen, "PLA's Shock and Awe Warfare Is Taiwan's Biggest Threat, Adjustment in Military Planning [Zhonggong zhenshe duitai weixie zui da, guojun niding zuozhan jihua]," Central News Agency [Zhongyangshe], May 5, 2004.

In the context of the evolving PRC military threat and these basic planning assumptions, Taiwan is taking important steps to deter PRC use of force and defend itself should deterrence fail. The armed forces are improving their war reserve stocks, investing in a defense industrial base, advancing their ability to carry out joint operations, and strengthening their personnel system for both active and reserve forces. In part, these investments will help to mitigate Taiwan's declining advantages.

Taiwan is in the midst of significant changes to its armed forces, particularly in the area of personnel. Taiwan has planned since 2010 to transition from a conscription force to an all-volunteer force—a plan originally scheduled for completion by the end of 2014 but recently postponed until at least the end of 2016 and perhaps beyond.[5] At the same time, Taiwan is reducing its active-duty force from 275,000 to approximately 175,000 personnel to create a more streamlined military by 2019. While savings from a smaller armed force could theoretically cover increased compensation for volunteers, these savings may be insufficient to fund personnel costs for the all-volunteer force. Moreover, the transition to an all-volunteer force appears to be creating pressures on other areas of Taiwan's defense budget—leading to a reduction in funds available for force modernization, training, and maintenance. In addition to the competition for resources within the defense budget, the total defense budget has until recently been declining. Competing requirements within Taiwan's central government budget have resulted in a decline in its defense budget over the past decade from over 4 percent to just 2 percent of gross domestic product.[6]

Fiscal limitations and a reduced force structure, alongside growing personnel costs and increased PLA military capabilities, highlight the need for more innovative approaches to personnel management. One possible area of investment is the reserve force. Taiwan's defense establishment maintains a significant reserve force that can mobilize to augment active-duty personnel in the defense of Taiwan. While pub-

---

[5] "All Volunteer Military Plans Postponed," *Taipei Times,* August 27, 2015, p. 1.

[6] Bonnie Glaser and Anastasia Mark, "Taiwan's Defense Spending: The Security Consequences of Choosing Butter Over Guns," The Asia Maritime Transparency Initiative and the Center for Strategic and International Studies, March 18, 2015.

licly available sources are unclear regarding the plans for staffing the reserves in the future all-volunteer era, it appears that conscription will continue to apply for some time to those males who do not volunteer for active service.[7] Taiwan's force transformation program reduced compulsory military service for the reserve force from one year to four months of basic and specialized training prior to assignment to the reserve force, and the service does not necessarily have to be continuous. For example, a university student may divide his military service commitment into two eight-week periods over two consecutive summers to fulfill his service obligation. After that, the conscript will register with his local reserve command, where he will report for duty only once every two years for a mere five to seven days of refresher training. That equates to as little as 20 days of training spread out over eight years.[8] After eight years, conscripts will go into inactive reserve status, and Taiwan will call these inactive reservists back into service only in the event of a war. Noncommissioned officers (NCOs) and officers, in contrast to other reservists, continue to receive refresher training until age 50 and may stay in the system even longer if they reach a high rank.[9]

As the number of active-duty soldiers, sailors, airmen, and marines continues to decrease, Taiwan should reconceptualize its reserve force to ensure that reservists are properly trained and prepared for high-intensity combat. Taiwan theater commanders are likely to consider calling on their assigned reservist brigades for increasingly difficult missions. Given that reservists are now entering the force with reduced training time, during an invasion, a significant number of them may be unable to meet the basic demands of their commanders. Moreover, the demands placed on active personnel in low-density but high-value

---

[7] It is possible, and seems likely for the time being, that "all-volunteer" will apply only to the active force. See Kevin McCauley, "Taiwan Military Reform: Declining Operational Capabilities?" *China Brief*, Vol. 13, No. 12, June 7, 2013.

[8] Authors' discussions with Taiwan military authorities with direct access in Taipei, August 20, 2015.

[9] Authors' discussions with Taiwan military authorities with direct access in Taipei, August 20, 2015, and authors' discussions with Taiwan military authority with direct access in Washington, D.C., October 13, 2015.

positions in the new threat environment, such as pilots and information technology specialists, call for augmentation from reservists with levels of professionalism and training that are indistinguishable from that of their active-duty counterparts.

Taiwan defense planners can no longer count on a future PLA landing at only a limited number of preordained locations. On a hypothetical future D-day, landings might take place all around Taiwan and at all levels of depth. What level of combat capability and training is required for Taiwanese reservists if they increasingly take on combat roles? The current one-size-fits-all approach to reserve force refresher training may be appropriate for some noncombat support personnel in the system, but inadequate for maintaining the readiness of those who would actually see combat in the event of an all-out Chinese invasion, or for those who would need to fill low-density, high-value positions.

Reserves staff all of the infantry brigades that would defend beaches against PLA amphibious landing attempts, and reservists are required to bring active-duty units to full strength in wartime. Given Taiwan's ongoing but tumultuous force transformation, are reservists up to the task? If Taiwan's leaders expect the reserve force to mobilize to face an increasingly capable threat from the Chinese mainland, what are the most promising areas in which to invest in reserve force modernization and transformation? More specifically, the Office of the Under Secretary of Defense for Policy asked RAND to explore and assess the following areas:

- **Task 1. Assess current Taiwan reserve force structure, roles, and missions.** Based on publicly available research and expert discussions, assess current Taiwan reserve force structure, roles, and missions. Identify potential gaps in current capabilities to meet future threats.
- **Task 2. Analyze needed future capabilities.** Conduct a strategic-level analysis and make recommendations for future Taiwan reserve force roles, missions, and capabilities, based on the requirement to counter PRC advantages in air and maritime power-projection capabilities.

- **Task 3. Identify needed enablers.** Based on the results of Task 2, identify potential enabling capabilities and specialist units that Taiwan could incorporate into the reserve force structure. These enablers might include, but are not limited to, explosive ordinance disposal experts, logistics units, military police, engineers, and medical units and personnel.
- **Task 4. Summary and final recommendations.** Recommend reserve force transitional needs in the context of Taiwan's broader future force requirements.

We based this study on a comprehensive literature review and discussions with defense experts in Taiwan and the United States in the latter half of 2015.[10]

Chapters Two, Three, and Four address the first task, summarizing current reserve force structure, roles, missions, capabilities, and capabilities gaps. Chapter Five addresses the threat assessment and strategic-level analysis of the cross-Taiwan Strait balance required by Tasks 2 and 3. Chapter Six delineates the future force and key enabler recommendations based on this strategic analysis. Chapter Seven concludes the study with a summary of recommendations from previous chapters and the appendix, as well as a note highlighting the critical importance of reserve force reform, funding, and training to Taiwan security in an increasingly tenuous cross-Strait environment.

This report also includes an appendix with a brief comparative analysis of reserve force transformation in other countries (Finland, Singapore, Japan, and Georgia), in which we also recommend that U.S. and Taiwan decisionmakers take a closer look at the reserve forces of Switzerland and, especially, Israel to glean lessons potentially relevant to Taiwan reserve force reform.

---

[10] These expert discussions were held in accordance with a RAND Human Subjects Protection Committee Institutional Review Board determination of exemption under 32 CFR 219.101(B) (2). The Office of the Under Secretary of Defense for Personnel and Readiness Research Regulatory Oversight Office concurred with this exemption in a memo dated August 27, 2015.

CHAPTER TWO

Taiwan Reserve Force Structure

Taiwan organizes its reserve force into military and civilian components. This chapter focuses primarily on the former. During peacetime, the ROC Ministry of National Defense (MND) oversees the reserve force in conjunction with the executive branch of Taiwan's central government, the Executive Yuan. In the event of wartime mobilization, the MND takes the lead and assumes an increased level of command and control over assets that are under the purview of other government ministries in peacetime.[1] The MND Armed Forces Reserve Command manages Taiwan's military reserve system, headquartered in Taipei. The Reserve Command headquarters staff consists of approximately 400 personnel[2] organized into the following four departments (Figure 2.1):

1. **General Staff Office:** responsible for personnel, readiness training, logistics, mobilization, planning, and funerary services.
2. **Political Warfare Office:** responsible for comprehensive political warfare, propaganda and psychological warfare, defense and security, and military awards.
3. **Inspection Office:** responsible for military discipline inspection, supervision and standards development, and legal affairs.

---

[1] Authors' discussions with Taiwan military authorities with direct access in Taipei, August 20, 2015.

[2] Authors' discussions with Taiwan military authorities with direct access in Taipei, August 20, 2015.

Figure 2.1
MND Reserve Command Headquarters Organization Chart

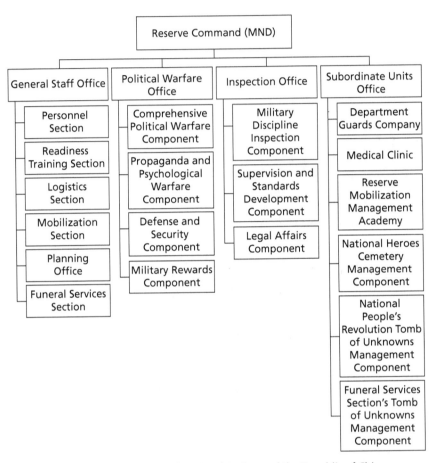

SOURCE: Adapted from Ministry of National Defense of the Republic of China,
"About Reserve Command," web page, no date-b.

4. **Subordinate Units Office:** comprised of components that include the Department Guards Company, the medical clinic, the Reserve Mobilization Management Academy, the National Heroes Cemetery Management Component, the National People's Revolution Tomb of Unknowns Management Component, and the Funeral Services Section's Tomb of the Unknowns Management Component.[3]

The Reserve Command oversees three regional reserve commands: the Northern Area Reserve Command, the Central Area Reserve Command, and the Southern Area Reserve Command. Each of these commands operates its own reserve training center and oversees a number of local municipal and county-level reserve commands.[4] The total manpower available to each regional and local reserve command is not publicly available, but numbers reflect population density. As such, the manpower available to the Northern Area Reserve Command is greater than the other two because of the large concentration of people in northern Taiwan.[5] Figure 2.2 illustrates the organizational structure of the overall MND reserve system.

Taiwan authorities oversee a large compulsory reserve system intended to mobilize 2.5 million men to augment its current active-duty (or full-time) force of approximately 215,000.[6] One newspaper, citing a Taiwan National Audit Office source, reports that, in 2014, Taiwan had 286,746 NCOs and 28,215 junior officers in the reserve

---

[3] Ministry of National Defense of the Republic of China, "About Reserve Command," web page, no date-b.

[4] See Ministry of National Defense of the Republic of China, no date-b.

[5] Authors' discussions with Taiwan military authorities with direct access in Taipei, August 20, 2015.

[6] The active-duty force number breaks down in the following manner: Army (including military police) 150,000; Air Force (including Air Defense Missile Command) 35,000; and Navy (including Marines) 30,000. For data on the size of the Taiwan active and reserve military force, see "Armed Forces: Taiwan," *Jane's Sentinel Security Assessment: China and Northeast Asia*, September 28, 2015, p. 1.

Figure 2.2
MND Reserve Command Organization Chart

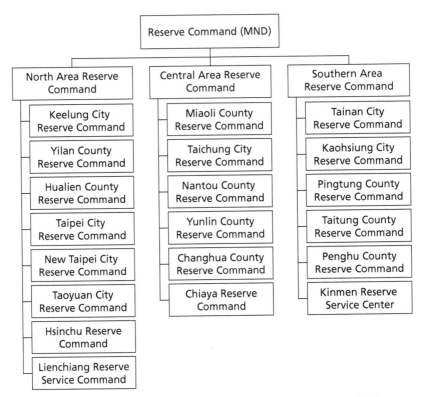

SOURCE: Adapted from Ministry of National Defense of the Republic of China, no date-b.
RAND RR1757-2.2

system.[7] In addition, Taiwan has nearly 1 million civil defense volunteers, who can mobilize to provide such military support activities as air raid defense, communications, firefighting, first aid, and traffic control.[8] Since Taiwan's total population is around 23.4 million, a conservative estimate is that approximately 15 percent of the population,

---

[7] Lee Hsin-fang, "Military Reservist Numbers Cut, Taiwan's Combat Power to See Gaps by 2020 [後備軍人遞減109年我軍戰力出現缺口]," *Liberty Times* [自由時報], July 30, 2015.

[8] Authors' discussions with Taiwan military authorities with direct access in Taipei, August 20, 2015.

and one man out of every four, is available for mobilization in the event of war.[9] By comparison, the reserve components of the United States Armed Forces comprise approximately 1.1 million service members, accounting for less than 0.4 percent of the total U.S. population.[10]

The majority of Taiwan's military reservists are ROC Army soldiers.[11] The ROC Navy, Marine Corps, and Air Force each have reserve units as well. The Navy (including the Marine Corps) reserve has approximately 60,000 personnel; the Air Force (and Air Defense Missile Command) has approximately 60,000 reservists.[12] Reserve units fall into four categories, which vary in terms of staffing, equipment, and readiness standards:[13]

- **A-Level** reserve units are infantry brigades manned, equipped, and maintained at the highest states of readiness. The ROC Army has eight or nine of these reserve brigades. These units are composed of many permanently assigned active-duty troops, and they would require only a relatively small number of supplementary reservists to mobilize for combat. These brigades are equipped with advanced weapons, including long-range artillery.
- **B-Level** reserve units are composed of active-duty personnel in the MND's professional military education system. For example, soldiers studying at the military academies and officers training

---

[9] This estimate is based on a conservative assumption that the total number of military reservists and civil defense reservists in Taiwan is 3.5 million. If this is correct, then Taiwan is poised to mobilize approximately 15 percent of its overall population, and approximately one in every four males. For Taiwan's population in 2015, see "Taiwan Population 2015," *World Population Review*, September 13, 2015.

[10] Lawrence Kapp and Barbara Salazar Torreon, *Reserve Component Personnel Issues: Questions and Answers*, Washington, D.C.: Congressional Research Service, June 13, 2014, p. 5. For population data, see U.S. Census Bureau, "U.S. and World Population Clock," 2016.

[11] "Armed Forces: Taiwan," 2015, p. 1.

[12] "Armed Forces: Taiwan," 2015, p. 1.

[13] The following section, unless otherwise noted, is based on the authors' discussions with U.S. military representatives and Taiwan military authorities in Taipei, August 19–20, 2015, and in Washington, D.C., October 13, 2015.

in the command academies are B-Level reservists. They require more time and effort to mobilize than A-Level brigades do.

- **C-Level** reserve units are local infantry brigades. The ROC Army has approximately 22 of these reserve brigades. Each brigade, once mobilized, has three to five battalions of infantry and one battalion of field artillery. They require more time and effort to mobilize than B-Level brigades do.
- **D-Level** reserve units are composed of forces drawn from reserve mobilization officer training centers directly subordinate to the MND Reserve Command. These reserve forces, once mobilized, would comprise at least two or three infantry brigades in strength, but would not have organic artillery support.[14]

The structure of Taiwan's military reserve force reflects the various roles and missions assigned to subordinate units. Units tasked with more demanding missions are at relatively higher readiness levels and organized accordingly. Units responsible for carrying out less demanding missions are structured and equipped to reflect lower levels of responsibility. We describe the roles and missions of Taiwan's military reserve forces in the next chapter.

---

[14] Author's electronic discussion with Taiwan military authority, August 28, 2015.

CHAPTER THREE

Reserve Force Roles and Missions: From Peacetime Through Mobilization to War

Taiwan's Reserve Command has both peacetime and wartime missions. Taiwan faces an adversary (the PRC) that is close to its territory and equipped with ballistic missiles and other weapons intended to minimize warning time. Making matters worse, PLA doctrine emphasizes rapid, overwhelming missile and air strikes against key targets on Taiwan. Potential PLA use of force requires that Taiwan maintain the capacity to mobilize its reserve force rapidly and under stressful conditions.[1]

In peacetime, the command is responsible for managing the tri-service reserve system, organizing and training reserve units, recruiting new talent, and preparing, certifying, and executing mobilization plans.[2] The Reserve Command supports humanitarian assistance and disaster relief operations, although these missions usually fall to regular army units.[3] Among its peacetime missions, the Reserve Command most heavily emphasizes preparing and certifying mobilization plans. Reserve units at the local and regional level, as well as civilian contractors, are responsible for preparing mobilization plans in accordance with national plans prepared by the Reserve Command, and the com-

---

[1] Ministry of National Defense of the Republic of China, "About Reserve Command: Missions," web page, no date-a; authors' discussions with Taiwan military authorities with direct access in Taipei, August 20, 2015.

[2] See Ministry of National Defense of the Republic of China, no date-a.

[3] Ministry of National Defense of the Republic of China, no date-a; and authors' discussions with Taiwan military authorities with direct access in Taipei, August 20, 2015.

mand certifies these plans at the national level through inspections and exercises.[4]

In addition to its planning functions, Taiwan's Reserve Command is responsible for providing refresher training for more than 2 million reservists to ensure that they maintain basic military skills and the ability to mobilize rapidly and effectively. Training generally consists of five days of basic drills once every two years. NCOs receive one extra day of training, or six days of training every two years; officers typically receive two extra days of training, or seven days total.

The Reserve Command is also responsible for the provision of intensive prewar training in the event of an emergency call-up. As mentioned earlier, a basic defense planning assumption is that Taiwan will have about four weeks' warning prior to a PLA amphibious invasion. The Reserve Command would use this time, in part, to prepare mobilized reservists for combat.[5] This warning would probably not apply to more limited Chinese military strikes, meant to punish Taiwan rather than to force unification—scenarios that would certainly stress Taiwan's mobilization system but not require the same level of reserve force deployment to defensive positions.

The Reserve Command is further responsible for planning, inspecting, assessing, and certifying Taiwan's national capacity to mobilize defense assets. This includes preparing for the mobilization of defense industrial facilities, critical infrastructure, and relevant private companies. To support wartime needs, civilian factories would transform production lines for military use. Weapon factories and other suppliers of military equipment would ramp up their activities to increase

---

[4] A recent example of a mobilization exercise can be found in Taiwan press releases, such as the recent *China Post* description of Tung Hsin no. 28 exercise—see "MND Mobilizes Reservists for Tung Hsin Exercise," *China Post,* August 22, 2016.

[5] Authors' discussions with Taiwan military authorities with direct access in Taipei, August 20, 2015. Note that this assumption is for a high-end invasion scenario, not for a punitive strike, which Beijing could order and the PLA could execute with little warning. In an invasion scenario, Taiwan planners assess that PRC mobilization activity would provide about 30 days of warning before the onset of missile and air strikes preceding the invasion. This assessment also does not take into account that decreased warning times may result from increased levels of PLA training activity and readiness posture.

production output rapidly.[6] The Reserve Command would also requisition large numbers of dual-use properties and vehicles. Civilian assets in the reserve system include 10,000 fixed facilities, 2,000 pieces of heavy machinery, 300 fishing boats, 60 aircraft, and 50 ships.[7]

In wartime, the Reserve Command is responsible for providing mobilized reserve brigades to operational commanders. Figure 3.1 delineates the primary military mobilization tasks, which, as the figure shows, involve both mobilizing military units, including material and personnel, and mobilizing both civilian and military industry to support military activities. The Reserve Command is additionally responsible for mobilizing and coordinating Taiwan's all-out defense efforts, as illustrated in Figure 3.2, which shows how the military mobilization works alongside civilian mobilization in a comprehensive mobilization process.

For Taiwan, mobilization entails more than just bringing latent military capabilities into action (Figure 3.2, right side). Taiwan's central administrative governing body, the Executive Yuan, and its directly subordinate ministries and local government departments (Figure 3.2, left side) will put their respective capabilities at the MND's disposal in the event of a conflict. The Reserve Command plays the role of coordinator (in the role of the All-Out Combat Power Coordination Organization depicted in the center of Figure 3.2).[8] Mobilization is an all-out national defense effort that affects the entire population, which includes the planned integration of civil defense units and civilian contractor assets into military operations for homeland defense.[9]

The sections to follow consider first the role of civilian ministries in mobilization, then highlight missions for each reserve military service component as they transition through mobilization to war.

---

[6] Chen Qing-lin, *National Defense Education: Defense Mobilization* [全民國防教育防衛動員], New Taipei City: New Wun Ching Development Publishing, 2013, pp. 12–13.

[7] "Armed Forces: Taiwan," 2015, p. 6.

[8] Authors' discussions with Taiwan military authorities with direct access in Taipei, August 20, 2015.

[9] Authors' discussions with Taiwan military authorities with direct access in Taipei, August 20, 2015.

Figure 3.1
Taiwan Reserve Command's Military Mobilization Tasks

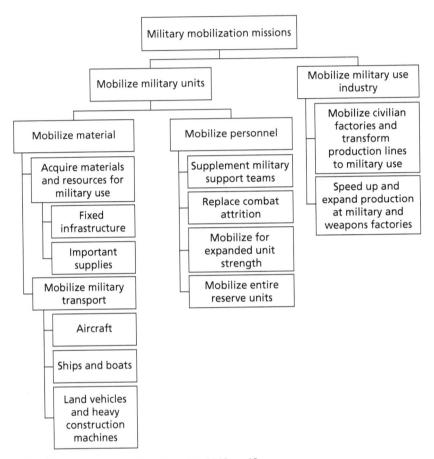

SOURCE: Adapted from Chen Qing-lin, 2013, p. 13.

RAND RR1757-3.1

Civilian Mobilization Missions

At the heart of the all-out defense strategy is Taiwan's Executive Yuan, which is responsible for mobilizing civilian assets within the government bureaucracy to support military operations. Each cabinet-level ministry or administration under the Executive Yuan has one or more missions assigned to it. Each component of the government bureaucracy, from the national level to the municipal level to the local level,

Figure 3.2
All-Out Defense Mobilization Process and Missions Chart

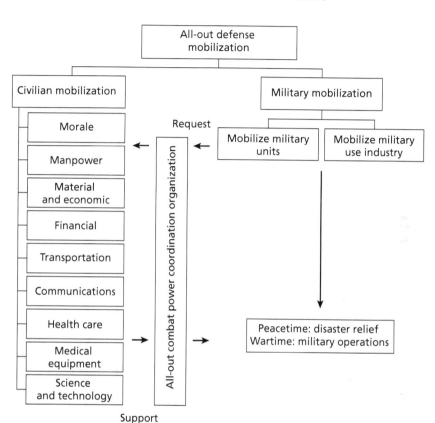

SOURCE: Adapted from Chen Qing-lin, 2013, p. 11.
RAND RR1757-3.2

must draw up and regularly update its own detailed mobilization plan. The Executive Yuan integrates and certifies these plans through regular training drills. The following offers a breakdown of civilian organizations and missions assigned:[10]

- **The Ministry of Education** is responsible for mobilizing public morale or "spiritual resources" across Taiwan. During peace-

---

[10] The following section, unless otherwise noted, draws from Chen Qing-lin, 2013, pp. 11–13.

time, this involves providing patriotic national defense education courses to students and organizing and participating in air defense drills. During wartime, the Ministry of Education is tasked with providing student labor and school campuses to support military operations.

- **The Ministry of the Interior** is responsible for mobilizing professional technical personnel, civil defense personnel, volunteer firefighters, humanitarian assistance and disaster relief groups, and other volunteer and charitable organizations. During peacetime, the ministry is in charge of the inspection, assessment, and organization of the above groups and their resources. During wartime, the Ministry of the Interior mobilizes civil defenses to support military operations. In addition, it oversees school youth groups that would mobilize to support civil defense operations.

- **The Ministry of Economic Affairs** is responsible for mobilizing critical supplies, personnel, and other resources, including those related to the protection and repair of Taiwan's oil, electricity, and water infrastructure.

- **The Ministry of Finance** is responsible for mobilizing financial resources to support national mobilization. The Ministry of Finance's mission is to plan and budget Taiwan's war costs, stabilize wartime finances, and use its foreign reserves and other assets.

- **The Ministry of Transportation** is responsible for mobilizing national transportation assets, including trucks, buses, and tractor-trailers; ships and boats; aircraft; and heavy engineering machinery. The Ministry of Transportation is further responsible for mobilizing national communications assets.

- **The Health Administration** is responsible for mobilizing Taiwan's medical personnel, facilities, medicines, and related supplies. Its mission is to plan for the wartime establishment of emergency medical units, triage, and dispersal operations, and to prepare emergency stocks of medical supplies.

- **The National Science Council** is responsible for mobilizing Taiwan's science and technology sectors, including high-tech manufacturers, academia, and research units. Its mission is to plan for the wartime establishment of science and technology talent centers to support the war effort.

Military Mobilization Missions

Ground Force Missions

Military units within the reserve system would play a wide range of roles in the event of war.[11] Army reserve units would have four main missions: (1) coastal defense, (2) key point defense, (3) defense in depth, and (4) counterattack. Coastal and key point defense missions belong primarily to C-Level reserve units organized into brigades for static defense missions. These reserve brigades would muster at predesignated reserve bases on Taiwan and the offshore islands. Units would draw on stored guns, ammunition, mortars, artillery, and other equipment. Some units would deploy to fortified coastal positions, while others would staff high-priority locations and facilities inland. For example, C-Level brigades augment the defense of bridges, tunnels, highway intersections, ports, airfields, and urban areas. Lacking the capabilities and readiness of other reserve units, C-Level reserve brigades would defend their own hometowns and thus have the advantage of local knowledge and popular support. They would also be fighting alongside active-duty units with advanced training and experience.

The Army's B-Level reserve units are responsible for tasks of low-to-intermediate-level difficulty in wartime. Some would defend fortified landing sites. Others would defend frontline military facilities that the PLA might attempt to capture. B-Level reserve units would also bolster regular combat units to compensate for combat attrition. For example, personnel from the Political Warfare Academy at the MND's Fu Hsing Kang College would deploy to the field to augment psychological warfare and counterintelligence units. The Taiwan Army's armor and artillery academies would mobilize their tanks and guns to bolster active brigades along the coast.

The Army's A-Level reserve units have the most demanding wartime missions. The Reserve Command designates A-level units for integration into regular ROC Army defense-in-depth and counterattack missions. These operations would be especially important if PLA forces succeeded in landing and consolidating coastal lodgments on Taiwan.

---

[11] This section, unless otherwise noted, draws from the authors' discussions with U.S. military representatives and Taiwan military authorities in Taipei, August 19–20, 2015.

A-Level reserve units would undertake specialized missions, based on their professional skill sets, to repel an invasion quickly. Active and reserve Marine Corps brigades have similar missions. Sometimes referred to as "strategic reserve" brigades, these army and marine units appear to be specifically tasked with destroying PLA assault groups at the Port of Taipei, the Tamsui River delta, the Taoyuan plain, and other locations before they could threaten Taipei.[12]

Navy and Air Force Missions

Navy reservists are responsible for mustering at their local naval bases, where they would assume a variety of base-support missions, depending on their individual skill sets. Naval reserve officers and NCOs would staff retired or mothballed ships that would reenter service in a wartime emergency.[13] Naval reservists also augment coastal mine-laying missions.[14] Air Force reservists are responsible for base service missions. When mobilized, they would bolster airbase perimeter defenses, air defenses, rapid runway repair teams, and maintenance units. The ROC Air Force does not maintain reserve officers to serve as pilots in wartime.[15]

Summary

The comprehensive nature of the roles and missions assigned to units within the MND's Reserve Force and the Executive Yuan, and their

---

[12] Authors' discussions with U.S. military representatives in Taipei, January 8, 2015, and July 3, 2015. See also "Reserve Mobilization: Counterattack after Tamsui Raid and Taipei Port Attack [後備動員淡水反突擊台北港反擊]," *Defence International* [全球防衛雜誌], No. 362, October 2014, pp. 36–43; and Chen Kuo-ming and Hwang Lin-chien, "The 29th Hankuang Exercise: Comprehensive Tri-Service Exercise of Important Objectives [漢光29號演習系列: 三軍重要項目總體檢]," *Defence International* [全球防衛雜誌], No. 345, May 2013, pp. 49–50.

[13] Authors' electronic discussions with Taiwan military authorities, August 28, 2015.

[14] Authors' discussions with Taiwan military authority in Williamsburg, Va., October 5, 2015.

[15] Authors' discussions with Taiwan military authority in Arlington, Va., September 2, 2015.

affiliates and subordinates, reveal the high degree of importance Taiwan places on being able to mobilize every facet of its national strength to counter its much larger adversary. It also highlights the primary role the Reserve Force plays in Taiwan's ability to mobilize comprehensively. The next chapter will discuss, to the limited extent that we can know or surmise outside of an actual conflict, the capabilities of Taiwan's Reserve Force.

CHAPTER FOUR

Reserve Force Capabilities

So far, this report has explored the organizational structures, roles, and missions of Taiwan's reserve force. Even though Taiwan's security concerns naturally preclude candor regarding certain aspects of its reserve force, the layout of the system itself is clear. Capabilities, on the other hand, are much more elusive and difficult to assess. They defy effective modeling because information about many factors is unavailable and it is difficult to quantify the quality of the force, particularly when under the stress of war. Moreover, our imperfect understanding is subject to biases inherent in our limited sources of information. We will not know Taiwan's reserve force capabilities until there is a war to test them. Nonetheless, based on the information that is available, we will address, in this chapter, three questions critical to characterizing Taiwan's reserve force capabilities:

1. Does Taiwan's reserve force appear to have the capability to mobilize for war quickly?
2. Does Taiwan's reserve force appear to have the capability to carry out its stated missions effectively?
3. Does Taiwan appear to be on the right track to maintain and improve its reserve force capabilities to keep up with the changing threat environment?

The chapter concludes with a brief discussion of capability gaps and challenges.

Characterizing Taiwan's Reserve Force Capabilities

Capability to Mobilize

The MND Reserve Command and the Executive Yuan place an extraordinarily high priority on mobilization. Taiwan has not reduced mobilization budgets in spite of the otherwise across-the-board cuts undertaken by the Taiwan military as part of its force transformation. Military units involved in certifying and executing mobilization plans have been spared from cuts, and some reserve brigades have seen their budgets increase, albeit modestly. As a result, Reserve Command officers express a strong confidence that within 24 hours of Taiwan's president issuing the relevant orders, the MND and the Executive Yuan could execute those orders to begin mobilizing the country. These officers believe this will be true even in the event that attacking PLA forces knocked out Taiwan's power grid and/or temporarily paralyzed electronic communications.[1]

Some U.S. military officers familiar with defense processes and authorities on Taiwan also assess that Taiwan's civilian and military leaders could set the mobilization process in motion rapidly in the event of impending conflict. One officer stated that he was impressed with the amount and frequency of planning, coordination, and contacts between the MND and logistics contractors and other civilian groups. Another American military authority said that every piece of equipment, including buses and bulldozers on Taiwan, was "tagged" or registered with a mobilization number. Moreover, the MND conducts monthly outreach to civilian contractors to certify its ability to call up their reserve services rapidly in a conflict.

Detailed priority lists of units and equipment for mobilization exist at all levels of government, and these lists include assigned responsibilities. According to one U.S. officer, "the Taiwanese would all fight and fight well. Despite political party differences, the population has a shared identity because of China's efforts to marginalize them in the

---

[1] Authors' discussions with Taiwan military authorities with direct access in Taipei, August 20, 2015.

international community. . . . The Taiwanese are very resilient."[2] While shortcomings exist, anecdotal evidence and public reports of recent call-up exercises suggest that Taiwan likely does have the capability to mobilize its reserve force for conflict.[3]

Capability to Effectively Carry Out Stated Missions

Since Taiwan's reserve force is made up primarily of conscripts, some soldiers and officers, both active duty and reserve, question whether current training rotations are sufficient preparation for combat. One Army reserve NCO expressed doubt that his unit's refresher training was serious and worthwhile. While proud of his national service, he felt a sense of disappointment that his unit, which had a combat arms mission, did not undergo more frequent and realistic training.[4] Air Force and Navy officers discussing this matter expressed confidence that reservists in each of their services could effectively carry out non-combat missions, such as logistics support or mine laying. They were skeptical, however, that infantry reservists received sufficient training to prepare them for combat operations in a high-intensity fight with an invading Chinese force.[5]

Some active-duty Army officers serving in the Reserve Command expressed more optimistic views. From their perspective, the sheer size of the reserve force ready for mobilization means that the Taiwan Army would be able to defend against landing Chinese forces at every conceivable point.[6] One senior officer emphasized the highly limited size of the battlespace and the care taken to match reserve units with missions

---

[2] Authors' discussions with U.S. military officer with direct access to Taiwan military authorities, in Taipei, August 20, 2015.

[3] For reports on reserve force mobilization exercise results, see "Reserve Mobilization: Counterattack After Tamsui Raid and Taipei Port Attack," 2014, pp. 36–43; and Chen Kuo-ming and Hwang Lin-chien, 2013, pp. 49–50.

[4] Authors' discussions with Taiwan military reservist in Arlington, Va., September 9, 2015.

[5] Authors' discussions with Taiwan military authorities in Arlington, Va., September 2, 2015, and in Williamsburg, Va., October 5, 2015.

[6] Authors' discussions with Taiwan military authorities in Taipei, August 20, 2015. Note that Taiwan authorities in this discussion did not address the changing nature of potential landing operations, where PLA air and missile operations likely would inflict heavy casual-

appropriate for their levels of training. He stated that Taiwan has been planning and preparing for this fight for decades. Moreover, he felt that basic infantry skills would suffice because many reserve force missions are limited. Professional, active-duty units would be doing the bulk of the fighting, and reservists would be simply augmenting the defense of their hometowns.[7] Nonetheless, one officer noted that "logically speaking, less time spent training will equate to less combat capability."[8]

Capability to Keep Up with the Changing Threat Environment

Taiwan's reserve force capabilities appear to be keeping pace with many, but not all, aspects of the changing threat environment. On the positive side of the ledger, Taiwan has demonstrated the capacity to mobilize its military and society to respond to both man-made and natural disasters. Indeed, U.S. and Taiwan experts highlighted Taiwan's experience and capabilities in handling natural disasters as indicative of reserve force capabilities, since those responses draw on the country's national civil-military reserve and mobilization system.[9] One U.S. military source noted Taiwan's experience with a "Katrina-sized typhoon event" in early August 2015. Unlike the response to Hurricane Katrina, however, Taiwan was able to repair millions of power and water outages within 24 hours and fully recover from the "super typhoon" within days.[10]

Armed conflicts and natural disasters share common features, including "a large impact zone with limited access, advantages of early warning, imperative of protecting strategic assets, and coordination of rescue and relief efforts that will require detailed planning, surveillance and warning, effective and survivable communications systems

---

ties on both Taiwan active and reserve forces prior to landing operations (see discussion in Chapter Five of this report).

[7] Authors' discussions with Taiwan military authorities in Washington, D.C., October 13, 2015.

[8] Authors' discussions with Taiwan military authorities in Taipei, August 20, 2015.

[9] Authors' discussions with U.S. military representatives and Taiwan military authorities in Taipei, August 19–20, 2015.

[10] Authors' discussions with U.S. military representative in Taipei, August 19–20, 2015.

and rapid emergency response capabilities."[11] By this measure, Taiwan's record of accomplishment of responding to natural disasters suggests that it is also well prepared for man-made disasters. Indeed, MND publications frequently link the two.[12]

However, the PLA is rapidly modernizing, with the objective of being able to project overwhelming force across the Taiwan Strait. While most analysts assess that the PLA's amphibious force would be hard-pressed to deliver the troops needed to overwhelm Taiwan defenses in a massive landing operation, current evidence suggests that the PLA is becoming more proficient in the use of helicopters, airborne forces, hovercraft, and ground effect vehicles (or "sea skimmers") to augment the amphibious force in future cross-Strait operations.[13] The PLA is also improving its special operations capabilities with a Taiwan scenario in mind.[14] When combined with traditional landing operations, and the missile and air strikes that would precede them, these threat elements would likely complicate Taiwan defense planning, especially as the overall balance of air and naval power continues to shift in China's favor.

While areas for improvement exist, especially training, progress may be constrained by factors outside of the control of the MND Reserve Command and Executive Yuan. We will briefly consider this issue in the next section.

---

[11] Mark A. Stokes and Tiffany Ma, *Taiwan, the People's Liberation Army, and the Struggle with Nature,* Arlington, Va.: Project 2049 Institute, May 2011, p. 2.

[12] For example, see Ministry of National Defense of the Republic of China, *Quadrennial Defense Review,* Taipei, March 2013, pp. 58–62; and Chen Qing-lin, 2013.

[13] For example, see Yang You-hung, "Research into Communist Military's Joint Island Landing Offensive Campaign Capabilities [共軍聯合島嶼進攻戰役能力研究]," *Reserve Force Journal* [後備半年刊], No. 88, October 2013; and Tsai Ho-Hsun, "Research on the Communist Military's Division Landing Operations [共軍師登陸作戰之研究]," *Army Studies Bimonthly* [陸軍學術雙月刊], Vol. 50, No. 537, October 2014.

[14] Kevin McCauley, "PLA Special Operations: Combat Missions and Operations Abroad," *China Brief,* Vol. 15, No. 17, September 3, 2015.

Potential Gaps and Future Challenges

As Taiwan reduces mandatory military service times and moves gradually toward an all-volunteer military, the reserve force could begin to face gaps in both quantity and quality of personnel. Taiwan, like other societies in Asia and Europe, suffers from a low birth rate. Indeed, it is one of the world's most rapidly graying societies. As the youth population declines, so will the workforce available for military service, something that will cut into the number of reservists available for combat by 2020.[15]

A professional military with highly trained and well-equipped forces could compensate for the expected reductions. In modern warfare, quality often is valued over quantity. However, Taiwan faces three related challenges regarding future force quality. One is the Legislative Yuan's reluctance to increase defense spending at the expense of popular social welfare programs. The second is Taiwan's inability to acquire certain items of advanced weaponry from the United States to modernize its aging equipment in a predictable process. Finally, despite Taiwan's extensive bilateral training exchanges with the United States, which are low-key and consistent with the unofficial relationship, Taiwan is constrained in its access to U.S.-led multilateral exercises that could help further improve its training.

From this perspective, Taiwan's international marginalization remains one of its most significant national security challenges, a problem that could worsen over time. Taiwan's military officers note, for example, that South Korea is comparable to Taiwan in terms of economic performance and political system. Yet while South Korea has access to U.S. AEGIS-equipped destroyers, F-35 fighters, and Abrams tanks, Taiwan's geostrategic position constrains acquisition of a number of such high-tech systems due to fears of Beijing's potential reaction.[16]

---

[15] Lee Hsin-fang, 2015.

[16] Authors' discussions with Taiwan military authorities with direct access in Washington, D.C., October 13, 2015. Most defense experts assess that the cross-Strait balance has shifted increasingly in Beijing's favor. Taiwan is reportedly ramping up indigenous programs in key air and maritime capabilities, but many of these capabilities will not accrue to the force for another decade or more, and may or may not fill critical capabilities gaps at that future point.

Moreover, Taiwan's isolation means its military cannot participate in multilateral military exercises that could provide it with best practices and insights into real-world combat techniques.[17] According to both American and Taiwan military officers, Taiwan's international position often has a negative effect on morale, something that has second-order effects on reserve force recruitment and retention.[18]

Barring developments that offer Taiwan a substantive role in the emerging Asian security architecture and that make available, with consistency and predictability, defense articles and services, the cross-Strait military balance could erode in the next decade, making Taiwan's defense challenges increasingly severe despite changes and reforms Taipei may undertake to improve its reserve force. Taiwan's future defense prospects hinge on strategic-level decisions as well as on-the-ground improvements. Our next section provides a strategic level analysis and explores what a future Taiwan reserve force might look like.

---

[17] Authors' discussions with Taiwan military authorities with direct access in Taipei, August 20, 2015.

[18] Authors' discussions with American and Taiwanese military authorities in Taipei, July 1–3 and August 19–20, 2015; and Arlington, Va., August 12, 2015.

CHAPTER FIVE

Strategic Analysis

Any discussion on strategy begins with a definition of the term itself. For this study, we use Aaron Friedberg's definition of *strategy* as "a plan for applying means to achieve ends in a competitive interaction involving the threat or actual use of force."[1] This view of strategy is concerned with understanding competitive situations in which there is a contest of adversary wills; where each side has different plans, goals, and interests; and where each side may react to what the other does. We define *means* as a credible ability to threaten or actually use force. Means are tangible and intangible resources used to advance the strategy. The *ends* are the strategic objectives. *Ways* connect the means and ends, providing the operational concepts and plans for applying means toward ends.[2] In this chapter, we examine the ends, ways, and means of cross-Strait strategic competition and analyze the strategic role of Taiwan's reserve force.

Strategic Ends

What are the envisioned ends of each side in the cross-Strait strategic competition? Beijing's long-term strategic goal is cross-Strait unification under the principle of "One Country, Two Systems," including recognition of a "One China" principle, under which Taiwan authorities cede

---

[1] Aaron Friedberg, "What Is Strategy?" American Academy of Strategic Education Lecture, Arlington, Va., October 17, 2015.

[2] Friedberg, 2015.

sovereignty to the PRC.[3] Taiwan's democratic system of government—an alternative to the PRC's authoritarian model—presents an existential challenge to CCP political authority. In the past, CCP has also emphasized Taiwan's geostrategic value, citing its position along the first island chain, the utility of the island in the PRC's desire to expand its maritime presence out to the second island chain, and the potential for foreign forces to use Taiwan as a base against China.[4]

Unification could take many forms, but the PRC maintains use of force as an option to deter the permanent legal separation of Taiwan from the mainland and to coerce governing authorities into a political settlement on Beijing's terms. The PRC claims that Taiwan is an inalienable part of China and has outlined conditions for use of force to unify Taiwan with the mainland, including if Taiwan declares independence, is occupied by a foreign country, or if it indefinitely refuses the peaceful settlement of cross-Strait unification through negotiation. At its most basic level, debates surround whether the most likely course of action could be some use of coercion short of a full-scale invasion or an actual invasion of Taiwan.

Taiwan's national security strategy seeks to sustain the ROC's continued existence as an autonomous and sovereign state under its constitutional framework. The development of a security strategy is complicated by divisions within Taiwan over the long-term relationship with mainland China—including competing objectives related to unification, maintenance of the status quo, or formal independence—as well as the pace of current interactions. Taiwan's national security strategy relies on a variety of instruments—political, military, economic, and cultural—in order to guarantee its survival.

---

[3] Central People's Government, People's Republic of China, *The One-China Principle and the Taiwan Issue*, 2000; and "Full Text of Anti-Secession Law," *People's Daily*, March 14, 2005.

[4] Among various sources, see Zhu Feng, "Why Taiwan Really Matters to China," *China Brief*, Vol. 4, No. 19, September 30, 2004; Richard C. Bush, *Untying the Knot: Making Peace in the Taiwan Strait*, Washington, D.C.: Brookings Institution Press, 2005; Alan Wachman, *Why Taiwan? Geostrategic Rationales for China's Territorial Integrity*, Stanford, Calif.: Stanford University Press, 2007; Robert D. Kaplan, "The Geography of Chinese Power," *Foreign Affairs*, May/June 2010; and Information Office of the State Council, People's Republic of China, *China's National Defense in 2010*, March 2011.

Within the military context, Taiwan seeks to deny the PLA the ability to occupy and hold the island. Taiwan's MND has principal responsibility for ensuring the country's survival. The MND defines its strategic ends as preventing war, ensuring homeland defense, and responding rapidly to a crisis; avoiding confrontation; and supporting regional stability.[5] Taiwan might therefore be what strategist B. H. Liddell Hart calls a "status quo" state because it is content with its existing territorial borders and concerned only with preserving its security and maintaining its democratically elected government.[6] Taiwan can achieve its strategic objective by deterring PRC leaders from using force to settle political disputes. Taipei advances its strategy by convincing Beijing that the costs of any conflict would outweigh desired benefits.[7]

Strategic Ways and Means

Having established the ends that each side is seeking (the "what"), we can now consider the ways that each side plans to achieve its ends (the "how") and the specific capabilities or means, real or perceived, that underpin the ways in which each side intends to achieve its strategic ends. Over the past decade, cross-Strait relations have been relatively stable while Beijing pursues a preferred path to peaceful unification, through strengthened economic and cultural ties. Because Beijing does not ultimately trust in the inevitability of a peaceful way to the PRC's desired end state, PRC leaders have sharpened the military tools in their toolbox to coerce or compel Taiwan to accede to their demands if required. Likewise, Taiwan has plans in place to defend against a range of PRC attacks.

---

[5] Ministry of National Defense of the Republic of China, *Republic of China National Defense Report 2015* [中華民國104年國防報告書], October 2015, p. 67.

[6] B. H. Liddell Hart, *Strategy: Second Revised Edition*, New York: Meridian, 1991, p. 355.

[7] Among various sources, see U.S. Department of Defense, *Report to Congress on Implementation of the Taiwan Relations Act*, Washington, D.C., 1999; and Ministry of National Defense of the Republic of China, 2013.

PRC Strategies

The PRC has a number of military courses of action available. An amphibious invasion to compel unification is the least likely yet most dangerous scenario. PRC decisionmakers could also resort to coercive uses of force short of a full-scale invasion, in order to achieve limited political objectives. Coercive strategies might include a blockade intended to economically pressure Taiwanese decisionmakers to consent to Chinese demands for unification negotiations; a punitive joint fire-strike campaign combining missile and air strikes against key Taiwan military and possibly civilian targets to reverse an undesirable political action or trend on Taiwan; or a focused campaign to strike and topple Taiwan's central leadership in Taipei. However, we cannot predict the outcome of coercive campaigns with any degree of certainty.

While resolution of differences on Beijing's terms through peaceful means would be preferable to the PRC, China's leaders may perceive at some point that occupation of the island is the only means to achieve cross-Strait unification. A PLA joint island landing campaign, which represents the operational concepts for a full-scale invasion of Taiwan, hypothetically consists of three phases of operations.[8] The first phase would consist of joint air-sea blockades and joint strike (bombing) operations. In this phase, the PRC would seek to seize control over the information (electromagnetic), air, and sea domains by disabling Taiwan's critical infrastructure, air defenses, and maritime defenses.

The second phase of operations would be the main amphibious assault. This phase could involve assembling PLA amphibious assault groups in staging areas along the Chinese coast, loading them aboard transport ships, sailing to offshore rally points, crossing the Taiwan Strait, disembarking onto landing ships 25–50 kilometers off Taiwan, bombarding the coast, and executing amphibious landings at preselected beaches. The PLA could conduct airborne landings, helicopter assaults, and special operations raids in conjunction with beach landings. In this phase of operations, the PRC may seek to maintain elec-

---

[8] The following section on campaign plans, unless otherwise noted, draws from Ian Easton, *The Chinese Invasion Threat: Taiwan's Defense and American Strategy in Asia*, Arlington, Va.: Project 2049 Institute, forthcoming.

tromagnetic, air, and sea control while executing landings along Taiwan's coastline. The PLA's operational objectives could be to disable Taiwan's coastal defenses and then secure lodgments at beaches, ports, and airstrips at multiple points on Taiwan, especially those near Taipei.

The third phase of operations may be the final fight on Taiwan. Intense fighting in urban and mountain environments would define this phase. The PLA may attempt to rapidly build up its coastal lodgments, fight off counterattacks, break into the depths of Taiwan, capture the seat of government, and clear out the rest of the island. The PLA would seek to end the war in this phase. Its operational objective would be to defeat Taiwan's military around Taipei and clear out remaining defenders in cities, mountains, and offshore islands around Taiwan.

Defense of Taiwan

Taiwan's military authorities closely monitor PLA operational concepts regarding a full-scale invasion campaign, and make their own plans and preparations accordingly.[9] Security concerns naturally preclude any detailed public discussion regarding Taiwan's defense planning. It is possible, however, to form a general picture based on MND defense white papers and media reporting on Taiwan military exercises, which test combat readiness in the event of PLA attack. These sources indicate that Taiwan military plans for countering a PLA joint island landing campaign may envision three phases of operations. These plans likely assume a "worst-case" scenario wherein PRC counter-intervention efforts deterred, delayed, or in some way denied U.S and/or other international intervention. Phases and operations would thus adjust to take advantage of third-party support if and as it arrives.

---

[9] See Hsieh Chi-peng, "Research on Latest Communist Military Campaign Guidance [共軍新時期戰役指導之研究]," *Army Studies Bimonthly* [陸軍學術雙月刊], No. 536, August 2014, p. 35, written when the author was a reserve ROC Air Force Lt Col and instructor at the ROC National Defense University. See also Tsai Ho-shun, 2014, p. 61, written when the author was an ROC Army LTC serving in the ROC National Defense University Army Command Academy's Intelligence Cell. And see Yang You-hung, 2013, p. 109, written when the author was an ROC Army LTC serving as the commander of the Taoyuan County Reserve Command Post.

The first hypothetical phase of the defense of Taiwan would be what the MND refers to as *force preservation*.[10] This phase would involve deployment of military aircraft to hardened shelters and alternative operating locations, including civilian airports and highway runways scattered around the island.[11] Taiwan's naval fleet could sortie from ports and steam to secure maneuver areas.[12] Ground units, including mobilized reserve forces, would deploy to defend key geographic areas and critical infrastructure. Taipei would emphasize the wartime preservation of telecommunication nodes, transportation routes, energy reserves, water reservoirs, and electrical infrastructure.[13] In this phase, Taiwan would seek to ensure that its forces survived PLA first strikes and then rapidly recovered their combat power. Taiwan's operational objective would be to deny the enemy control over the electromagnetic, air, and sea domains.

The second phase of the defense of Taiwan could be what the MND refers to as *joint combat operations*.[14] This phase may consist of air, sea, and special operations strikes on a limited number of coastal targets judged essential to the PLA invasion.[15] If these strikes failed to disrupt PLA troop embarkation operations, Taiwan could then begin

---

[10] Ministry of National Defense of the Republic of China, 2015, p. 69.

[11] For example, see "2014 Spring Festival Combat Patrol: Tough Tri-Service Readiness Drills Held [2014春節戰鬥巡弋陸海空三軍精實戰力呈現]," *Defence International* [全球防衛雜誌], No. 354, February 2014, pp. 35–36. See also You Tai-lang, "Han Kuang Exercise: Back-Up Runway Landings Successful [漢光演習 副跑道降落圓滿達成]," *Liberty Times* [自由時報], April 18, 2012; and Fu S. Mei, "Operational Changes in Taiwan's Han Kuang Military Exercises 2008–2010," *China Brief*, Vol. 10, No. 11, May 27, 2010.

[12] "2014 Spring Festival Combat Patrol: Tough Tri-Service Readiness Drills Held [2014春節戰鬥巡弋陸海空三軍精實戰力呈現]," 2014, pp. 33–34.

[13] Authors' discussions with Taiwan military authorities with direct access in Taipei, August 20, 2015.

[14] Ministry of National Defense of the Republic of China, 2015, p. 68.

[15] See Zhou Yi et al., "Assessing Taiwan's Ballistic Missile and Cruise Missile Development [台湾弹道导弹与巡航导弹发展评析]," *Winged Missile Journal* [飞航导弹], No. 5, 2005, p. 29. For a more recent PLA analysis on Taiwan's strike capabilities, see Jiang Yanyu, ed., *A Military History of Fifty Years in the Taiwan Area 1949–2006* [台湾地区五十年军事史 1949–2006], Beijing: Liberation Army Press, 2013, p. 228. According to one senior ROC officer, Taiwan has carefully surveyed targets and planned counterstrike operations for neu-

layered (subsurface, surface, and air) interdiction attacks on the invasion fleet as it crossed the Taiwan Strait.[16] The main goal of this phase could be to sink major enemy amphibious ships before they reached operating points near Taiwan's coast. Failing that, the objective would be to sink incoming amphibious assault vehicles and tank landing ships as they approached beach-landing sites.[17] ROC forces would also defend against PLA transport planes and helicopters carrying airborne assault troops.[18]

The third phase of the defense of Taiwan could be what the MND refers to as *homeland defense operations*.[19] This phase of operations would revolve around the defense of beaches, ports, and airstrips, denying them to PLA assault groups. If PLA forces did manage to establish beachheads for follow-on reinforcements, the objective of this phase would be to launch multiple waves of counterattacks to surround and annihilate these forces along the coast.[20] In the event that enemy forces were able to hold lodgments and build up heavy forces, the ROC military would engage in a series of delaying actions in urban and mountain areas to force the PLA into a war of attrition.[21] Having

---

tralizing PLA coastal bases and supporting infrastructure within range. Author's discussions in Taipei, June 2014.

[16] For a detailed account, see "Penghu Wude Joint Counter Amphibious Exercise [澎湖五德聯信聯合反登陸操演]," *Defence International* [全球防衛雜誌], May 2013, pp. 32–40.

[17] "Penghu Wude Joint Counter Amphibious Exercise [澎湖五德聯信聯合反登陸操演]," 2013.

[18] For details on Taiwan's short-range air defense capabilities, see Kuo Wen-liang, *National Defense Education: Defense Science and Technology* [全民國防教育國防科技], Taipei: NWCD Publishing, 2014, p. 132.

[19] Ministry of National Defense of the Republic of China, 2015, p. 68. See also Liu Ching-jong, "Research on War Zone Unit Modularization for Homeland Defense [國土防衛中 作戰區部隊模組化之研究]," *Reserve Force Journal* [後備半年刊], April 2011, pp. 17–33.

[20] For example, see Liu Ching-jong, "Examining the Application of Mechanized Infantry in Future Defense Operations [機步部隊在未來防衛作戰運用之探討]," *Army Studies Bimonthly* [陸軍學術雙月刊], Vol. 49, No. 529, June 2013, pp. 4–22.

[21] See Yeh Chien-Chung and Chen Hong-diao, "Evaluating Infantry Unit Urban Warfare Training [步兵部隊城鎮作戰訓練之探討]," *Army Studies Bimonthly* [陸軍學術雙月刊],

fought to a standstill, Taiwan would then begin a final all-out counter-attack to repulse the invasion. If this failed, Taiwan's remaining government and military would have to retreat to the mountainous east coast of the island in an attempt to regroup.[22]

Cross-Strait Balance

The operational concepts and plans (ways), developed by the ROC and PRC governments to advance their relative position have a considerable effect on the strategic competition between the two nations. Both likely update these war plans on a regular basis according to the latest intelligence, force modernization, and lessons learned from training drills, exercises, and simulations. They provide a framework for each side as they assess where they are relative to the other and where they need to go in the future.

According to authoritative Taiwan and Western military assessments, there is no assurance that the PLA currently can successfully invade Taiwan, despite its two-decade buildup. This would be particularly true if the U.S. militarily intervened in the conflict and complicated or even denied the PLA the operational objectives in the phases of the joint island landing campaign. Yet the PLA's resources are expanding rapidly and continually, and its military capabilities are improving. Assuming that current trends continue, the Taiwan MND estimates that the PLA might have a credible capability to conduct a joint landing campaign to occupy Taiwan by 2020.[23] Little public information is available regarding the measures the MND uses and the factors it takes into account when forecasting future PLA means. However, if the MND is correct, then the PLA is steadily advancing toward its strategic objective. While growth of the PRC's defense budget has accelerated, Taiwan's has decreased, and, as noted earlier, most defense

---

No. 537, October 2014, pp. 23–34.

[22] Authors' discussions with Taiwan defense authorities in Hualien, July 2015. See also Jiang Yanyu, 2013, p. 84.

[23] Ministry of National Defense of the Republic of China, 2015, p. 57.

analysts assess that the balance of power in the Strait has shifted significantly in favor of Beijing.[24]

Assessments of the cross-Strait military balance have traditionally taken the form of "bean counting" exercises whereby defense budgets, manpower numbers, equipment stockpiles, weapon ranges, and other factors are compiled and compared. Often, these data points serve as inputs for computer simulations, command post exercises, and scripted drills. Units are assigned point values, and sophisticated algorithms calculate kill probabilities based on player moves. These exercises, simulations, and games have important value, but they miss other qualitative factors that history shows are important and often decisive for deciding strategic outcomes.

The most significant uncertainty, by far, concerns the involvement of the United States. The Taiwan Relations Act provides for security assistance in the provision of U.S. arms to Taiwan, and the United States could use the act to justify U.S. intervention on Taiwan's behalf in a conflict with China—though the law does not *require* military intervention by the United States in such a conflict. A number of diplomatic, military, and domestic political factors would determine the scope and alacrity of U.S. response, and uncertainty surrounding potential U.S. reactions has been a principal deterrent to escalatory behavior by both the PRC and Taiwan. In terms of Taiwan's strategic ends and the growing capabilities of the PLA, the prudent approach to self-defense demands Taipei's focus on deterring and, if required, countering Chinese invasion capabilities and operations—if for no other reason than to prevent a Chinese *fait accompli* and buy time for U.S. and/or other international actions to factor in.

Having briefly described the strategic ends, ways, and means of each side in the cross-Strait competition, we are now in a position to explore the question of where Taiwan's reserve force fits into the ROC government's self-defense strategy.

---

[24] Ministry of National Defense of the Republic of China, 2015, p. 58.

Taiwan's Reserve Force Strategy

The strategy driving Taiwan to maintain its large reserve force has several elements, but the overall thrust appears straightforward. Taiwan maintains the ability to mobilize at least 3.5 million military and civilian reservists, including approximately 2.5 million army soldiers, as a means to guarantee that it can overpower any invading force.[25] Island warfare in the Second World War first demonstrated the need for an attacking force to have a large numerical advantage in order to secure victory. A minimum three-to-one superiority became, and continues to be, considered orthodox amphibious warfare practice. The unique military geography of the Taiwan Strait battlespace, defined by rough seas, foul weather, high mountains, and dense cities, further advances the defender's advantage. These challenges suggest that a five-to-one advantage is a more realistic baseline for notional PLA planning purposes.[26]

The PLA has a total military force of 2.3 million, with a ground force of 1.6 million and approximately half a million additional reservists.[27] The PLA is the ultimate guarantor of CCP monopolization of political power. It serves to augment China's internal security forces and is often the first responder to any major natural disaster that could threaten the CCP's legitimacy. A considerable portion of the PLA focuses on and trains to defend China's 14 land borders. Much of the ground force is scattered across the depths of China for this mission, with units dedicated to potential border conflagrations involving India,

---

[25] Taiwan's civil-military reserve system includes approximately 2,480,000 ROC Army reservists, 60,000 Navy (including Marine Corps) reservists, and 60,000 Air Force (including Air Defense Missile Command) reservists. Taiwan also has nearly 1 million civil defense reservists and a large, but unknown, number of civilian contractor reservists. The total force is believed to be between 3.5 and 4 million. See "Armed Forces: Taiwan," 2015, p. 1; and Gao Guangdong et al., "Taiwan Reserve Force Overview [台军后备部队扫描]," *World Outlook* [世界展望], No. 534, February 2006, pp. 68–69.

[26] Authors' discussions with U.S. military representatives in Taipei on January 8, July 3, and August 19, 2015.

[27] The PLA has a conscript-heavy army of approximately 1,600,000, a navy of 235,000, an air force of 398,000, a strategic missile force of 100,000, and 510,000 reserves. See International Institute for Strategic Studies, *The Military Balance 2015*, Vol. 115, No. 1, 2015, p. 237.

Russia, North Korea, Vietnam, Myanmar, Mongolia, and others.[28] While the CCP would certainly mobilize all forces deemed necessary in the event of a Taiwan invasion, it would still be a challenge for the PLA to concentrate all of its power on the invasion of Taiwan. Moreover, Beijing plans to reduce the size of the PLA by 300,000 in the next few years, and cuts likely will hit the ground force particularly hard.[29]

If the PRC decided to invade Taiwan, it could perhaps allocate about 1 to 1.5 million active ground force troops for the mission. It might also mobilize all of its reserves and provide them for the invasion of Taiwan. In the unlikely event that the PRC could successfully mobilize such a large force without compromising the PLA's other core missions, it would have a notional invasion force of approximately 1.5 to 2 million troops.[30] This hypothetical attacking army would face a fully mobilized defending army of 2.5 million troops on Taiwan. Additionally, tens of thousands of marines and paramilitaries, and over 1 million civil defense personnel and civilian contractors, would augment the Taiwan Army.

The ROC Air Force, Missile Command, Navy, and Coast Guard likely will take a toll on any PLA invasion fleet, reducing Chinese effectiveness in projecting power across the Strait. However, even if a hypothetical attacking force of 1.5 to 2 million could be transported across the Strait and land on Taiwan in good order and relatively unscathed, Taiwan forces would still outnumber the PLA on the ground by a ratio of roughly five to four. The PLA would not have the needed numeri-

---

[28] Dennis J. Blasko, *The Chinese Army Today: Tradition and Transformation for the 21st Century*, 2nd edition, New York: Routledge, 2012, pp. 86–101.

[29] Edward Wong, Jane Perlez, and Chris Buckley, "China Announces Cuts of 300,000 Troops at Military Parade Showing Its Might," *New York Times*, September 2, 2015.

[30] The PLA Army has a number of key missions that likely would prevent commitment of the full force to the invasion, even in a campaign as risky to the regime as a Taiwan invasion would be. Among other missions, the Army would be responsible for protecting China's borders in other theaters of operation and for augmenting domestic security forces in maintaining internal order, particularly in urban areas and potentially unstable regions such as Xinjiang and Tibet. In addition, constraints on PRC strategic and operational lift, both maritime and air, significantly delimits troop transportation capacity. See Wong, Perlez, and Buckley, 2015.

cal advantage generally assumed essential for victory. In fact, the ROC Army, even in a highly forgiving (and unrealistic) scenario allowing for unlimited and unconstrained PLA transport capabilities, could outnumber it.[31]

This analysis, while overly simplistic, suggests that Taiwan's reserve force, and in particular its army reserve component, could provide the necessary means to achieve Taiwan's strategic ends. Given the risk to the regime in the event of failure, PLA planners tasked with assessing the cross-Strait balance in an invasion scenario probably will use conservative estimates regarding PLA force size and lift estimates. This would logically lead them to judge the invasion of Taiwan as too risky to execute. If that were the case, the size of Taiwan's reserve force, when mobilized, could be sufficient to deter Chinese aggression and safeguard ROC sovereignty. Yet evidence indicates that the PLA has not given up on developing options that include an invasion of the main island of Taiwan. To explore why this might be, let us first turn to the issue of how the PRC perceives Taiwan's reserve force.

---

[31] Most, if not all, publicly available Western assessments of Chinese amphibious lift capacity note that the PRC's fleet of amphibious vessels falls woefully short of the "full invasion" requirement. Even when augmented by airlift for its airborne forces, helicopter lift for air mobile forces, and merchant ships adapted for military use, the PRC would require a number of "turns" back and forth across the Strait to land anywhere near the number of forces considered in this brief overview. Loss of PRC amphibious and other lift assets due to Taiwan, and potentially U.S., operations during these "turns" would further exacerbate this lift problem. It is important to recognize, however, that China has vast ship-building capacity which can be turned to amphibious construction—this would not be an immediate answer in a crisis, but the PRC could address capacity shortfalls relatively quickly (perhaps in under two to three years). Among various sources assessing the PLA's amphibious landing capabilities, see Michael O'Hanlon, "Why China Cannot Conquer Taiwan," *International Security*, Vol. 25, No. 2, Fall 2000, pp. 51–86; and Michael S. Chase, Jeffrey Engstrom, Tai Ming Cheung, Kristen Gunness, Scott Warren Harold, Susan Puska, Samuel K. Berkowitz, *China's Incomplete Military Transformation: Assessing the Weaknesses of the People's Liberation Army*, Santa Monica, Calif.: RAND Corporation, RR-893-USCC, 2015.

PRC Views of Taiwan's Reserve Force

It is important to understand how the PRC views Taiwan's reserve force, as deterrence is subjective in nature. For example, if China's political-military leadership is unaware of the size and capabilities of Taiwan's reserve force, then this capability may have little deterrent effect. The PLA, as the armed wing of the CCP, might also choose to ignore any facts judged too politically inconvenient to face. Two questions are particularly relevant in analyzing the strategic value of Taiwan's reserve force. First, what effect, if any, does Taiwan's reserve force have on PRC strategy? Second, what does Beijing know about Taiwan's reserve force, and what impact does Taiwan's reserve force have on Beijing's military calculations of possible war outcomes?

Publicly available sources suggest that Chinese military analysts have watched Taiwan's reserve force developments with concern since at least the early-to-mid 2000s, when Taiwan's government began professionalizing the military. For example, one 2004 Chinese article focused on the remarkably large size of the Taiwan reserves, then thought to be 3.8 million strong, and discussed reserve force roles in beach defense, counter airborne landing, urban warfare, and electronic warfare operations.[32] A more detailed 2006 article emphasized the large size of the Taiwan reserves, then thought to be 4 million strong, and examined their organization, training, and mobilization procedures.[33] While both articles evinced concern at the size and growing capabilities of Taiwan's reserve force, they also expressed the view that Taiwan's reserve force lacked sufficient funding and training to present the PLA with a fundamental challenge in the near term.[34]

By 2007, a somewhat less sanguine view of Taiwan's reserve force seems to have developed in the PRC. According to one senior PLA analyst, Taiwan's reserve force was stronger as the result of Taiwan's

---

[32] Liu Jian, "Taiwan Military Reserve Force: Difficulties in Becoming Deciding Factor [台军后备部队难成气候]," *Journal of Cross-Strait Relations* [两岸关系], March 2004, pp. 30–31.

[33] Gao Guangdong et al., 2006, pp. 68–71.

[34] Gao Guangdong et al., 2006; Liu Jian, 2004.

military downsizing and modernization program. Noting newly created reserve units and mobilization procedures for responding to emergencies, the analyst concluded with some criticism regarding Taiwan reservist training, but also added that

> overall, the Taiwan military has built a concrete set of reserve force management and mobilization mechanisms. These are capable of meeting their needs in an environment whereby military reforms are continually advancing reserve force composition, equipment, and training.[35]

Another PLA publication expresses concern regarding Taiwan reserve force developments. Since the 1990s, Taiwan has undertaken a series of reforms that have increased the number of reservists that can receive refresher training every year.[36] These PLA analysts report that Taiwan has also improved its mobilization mechanisms, resulting in 97 percent full reserve brigade mobilization within 24 hours at emergency call-up drills.[37] However, the analysts point out perceived weaknesses of the reserve force as well. Taiwan's reservists, in the view of these PLA analysts, do not receive adequate training, which might reduce their expected combat performance. Although 30 days of annual training was initially mandated for Taiwan's reservists, this rule has been reduced over time so that reservists now only receive five to seven days of refresher training once every two years. According to these Chinese analysts, this equates to an average of only three and a half days of actual combat training once trainees complete administrative tasks and other duties.[38] Yet PLA writings view Taiwan's reserve

---

[35] Xu Zhong, "Analyzing Taiwan Military Reserve Force Building [析台军后备力量建设]," *China Militia* [中国民兵], No. 2, 2007, pp. 56–57. Note that Xu Zhong was then–Deputy Director of the Foreign Military Studies Department of the PLA Navy Command Academy.

[36] Jiang Yanyu, 2013, p. 237. This is an authoritative text that was produced in partnership with the PLA General Staff Department and assistance from the Academy of Military Science's Taiwan Strait Military Research Center, the National Defense University's Strategic Studies Department, and the State Council's Taiwan Affairs Office.

[37] Jiang Yanyu, 2013, p. 271.

[38] Jiang Yanyu, 2013, p. 157.

force training system as a somewhat peculiar exception to the rule. Overall, PLA writings characterize Taiwan's military training program as professional, rigorous, and steadily improving.[39]

The views of PLA analysts, however, are meaningless in the strategic sense if decisionmakers in Beijing do not share them. A review of authoritative Chinese writings reveals that Taiwan's reserve force developments, while apparently an important issue for military experts, do not factor into higher-level PRC assessments regarding Taiwan's military power.[40] Instead, Beijing appears to consistently pay attention to the following six issue areas: (1) Taiwan's leadership statements, (2) Taiwan's defense strategy, (3) Taiwan's military exercises, (4) Taiwan's weapon acquisition, especially U.S. arms sales, (5) Taiwan's exchanges with foreign militaries, and (6) Taiwan's military scandals and other issues that negatively affect morale.[41] PRC assessments of Taiwan military power do not mention reserve force issues, even in instances where assessments cover topics logically related to Taiwan's reserve force. As an example of this phenomenon, one authoritative PRC analysis reported on a Taiwan mobilization exercise but focused entirely on the civil defense component for responding to natural disas-

---

[39] Jiang Yanyu, 2013, pp. 157–161 and 266. See also Pan Shaoying and Zhang Yingzhen, eds., *Research on Foreign (and Taiwan) Army and Military Training* [外(台)军陆军军事训练研究], Beijing: Liberation Army Press, 2006, p. 328.

[40] See Bai Chun and Wu Junxi, "Overview of Taiwan Military Situation in 2013 [2013年台湾军事情况综述]," in National Taiwan Research Committee, ed., *Taiwan 2013* [台湾2013], Beijing: Jiuzhou Press, 2014, pp. 116–132; Bai Guangwei and Ren Guozheng, "An Overview of the Taiwan Military Situation [台湾军事情况综述]," in PLA Academy of Military Science Foreign Military Research Department, ed., *Annual Report on World Military Developments* [世界军事发展年度报告], Beijing: Military Science Press, 2013, pp. 254–264; Dong Yuhong and Fan Lihong, "Overview of Taiwan Military Situation in 2008 [2008年台湾军事情况综述]," in National Taiwan Research Committee, ed., *Taiwan 2008* [台湾2008], Beijing: Jiuzhou Press, 2009, pp. 271–285; and Wang Weixing, "Taiwan Military [台湾军事]," in Ning Sao, ed., *2006–2008 Research Report on Taiwan Strait Situation* [2006–2008年台海局势研究报告], Beijing: Jiuzhou Press, 2006, pp. 247–276.

[41] See Bai Chun and Wu Junxi, 2014, pp. 116–132; Bai Guangwei and Ren Guozheng, 2013, pp. 254–264; Dong Yuhong and Fan Lihong, 2009, pp. 271–285; and Wang Weixing, 2006, pp. 247–276.

ters.[42] Another similar assessment provided a detailed report on Taiwan's downsizing program and transformation toward an all-volunteer force but failed to address the impact on Taiwan's reserve force.[43]

The above suggests that PLA experts may assess that Taiwan's reserve force could pose a significant challenge at the operational and tactical level of warfare but does not play a role in higher-level PRC strategic thinking. As such, the existence of the Taiwan reserve force may have little or no value in deterring war, at least at the current time. The CCP Politburo Standing Committee and Central Military Commission are going to make future decisions regarding Taiwan based on the information (or disinformation) they see and care about. In the event of a crisis, if Beijing did not consider Taiwan's reserve force a major factor worth worrying about, the reserves would have failed to contribute to deterring PRC aggression.

These conclusions do not suggest that the Taiwan reserve force has no strategic value. The reserve force is a vital strategic means for helping ensure Taiwan's ends because it plays an essential role in repelling PLA ground and airborne forces in an invasion scenario. Nonetheless, any cross-Strait crisis or conflict that escalates to the point of a PLA invasion attempt likely would be catastrophic in terms of cost to the actors involved, and possibly to global security and economic stability. Even if Taiwan repulsed the Chinese invasion and the war resulted in a victory for the ROC military, the attack would damage or destroy many of Taiwan's cities, airports, and harbors, with high fatalities, including civilian fatalities, inflicted on both sides. This is why Taiwan military concepts of operations have traditionally sought to prevent war, or if that is not possible, keep fighting confined to offshore islands and other areas along the PRC coastline.[44] In the next chapter, we will explore potential pathways for increasing the Taiwan reserve force's strategic value in the years ahead.

---

[42] Bai Chun and Wu Junxi, 2014, p. 123.

[43] Bai Guangwei and Ren Guozheng, 2013, pp. 254–257.

[44] Ian Easton, *Able Archers: Taiwan Defense Strategy in an Age of Precision Strike*, Arlington, Va.: Project 2049 Institute, September 2014, p. 48.

CHAPTER SIX

Future Prospects and Recommendations

As the political-military challenge from the PRC grows in the years ahead, the reserve force may play a more prominent role in Taipei's strategic competition with Beijing. This section will explore how the reserve force could become an instrument of statecraft, with the role of preventing war and augmenting deterrence. Additionally, we will make recommendations for future Taiwan reserve force roles, missions, and capabilities, based on the requirement to counter PRC advantages in air and maritime power-projection capabilities.

The Deterrence Role

How might Taiwan use its reserve force for deterring future Chinese aggression? To explore this question, we considered ways Taiwan could use its reserves to both deter PRC use of force and defend the island should deterrence fail. For deterrence to be effective, Taiwan's reserve forces must enter into the use-of-force decision calculus of China's military and civilian leadership. As previously discussed, PRC analysts have noted improvements in Taiwan's reserve force posture related to reform efforts, but, overall, these analysts seem to focus on weaknesses of the force and tend to discount it as a significant factor in broad assessments of Taiwan military power. To change this perception, Taipei should first assess the ways in which reserve force developments could attract the attention of decisionmakers in Beijing and then develop the reserve force in such a way as to convince Beijing that Taiwan's reserve force represents a major unfavorable factor in CCP strategic calculations.

The reality is that Taipei is probably not going be able to get Beijing to focus on issues that it prefers not to notice. However, Taipei can get Beijing to notice issues it already monitors. As discussed in the previous chapters, Chinese writings suggest that Beijing pays attention to a specific, limited number of indicators related to Taiwan's military power. By connecting these specific indicators to the reserve force, Taiwan can elevate the reserves' strategic contribution in deterring Chinese aggression.[1]

Along those lines, there are practical steps Taiwan can take to advance the strategic value of its reserve force. We offer four recommendations in this area:

1. *Publicly highlight the reserve force in leadership statements, published defense strategy documents, and the Taiwan press.* Leadership statements should include those made by the president, presidential office spokesperson, high-ranking MND officials, and national security advisors. These statements should explain what the reserve force is, why it is important, and how it helps prevent or, if necessary, win war. To be effective, these statements should be positive, confident, and reassuring to people on Taiwan. Defense strategy documents, such as the MND's quadrennial defense review and its bi-annual defense white papers, should repeat these themes.[2] Taiwan could also hold mobilization exercises and emphasize in the media the role of reserve forces in these activities—reinforcing particularly improvements in reserve force readiness.

2. *Highlight the reserve force at Taiwan's annual HAN KUANG exercises.* In recent years, the TUNG HSIN and TZU CHIANG reserve mobilization exercises have been part of the national HAN KUANG exercises. However, Taiwan typically mobilizes

---

[1] See Easton, forthcoming.

[2] MND quadrennial defense reviews and white papers published to date offer low levels of transparency regarding the Taiwan reserve force. They do not clearly explain its roles, missions, and capabilities. See Ministry of National Defense of the Republic of China, 2015, pp. 112–113; and Ministry of National Defense of the Republic of China, 2013, pp. 58–62.

only a single brigade-sized unit each year, and these drills play a relatively minor role in the overall exercise. Future iterations of HAN KUANG could feature expanded reserve force mobilization components, with multiple brigades and tens of thousands of men simultaneously mobilized across Taiwan and its offshore islands. Reservists would then fully integrate into live-fire exercises alongside active-duty units. To highlight the important role of the reserve force, the MND could provide Taiwan's media with special access to some of these events. The larger the number of reservists involved, the more attention generated.

3. *Engage in military-to-military exchanges* with the U.S. Department of Defense, including the Office of the Secretary of Defense (OSD), the Joint Staff, and the U.S. Army, that directly relate to improving the reserve force. These exchanges could include discussions on military procurements, such as tanks, artillery pieces, anti-tank missiles, man-portable air defense systems, and mobile air-defense, specifically geared toward the Taiwan reserve force. Military-to-military exchanges should include visits of high-ranking officers from the ROC Reserve Command to the United States for discussions with the U.S. Army Reserve. For example, the United States could extend an invitation to the Reserve Force commander to visit the United States. The two sides could consider establishing a joint reserve force working group, managed on the U.S. side by the Office of the Assistant Secretary of Defense for Manpower and Reserve Affairs. To meet the growing military challenge from the PRC, creative engagement solutions are required. OSD has security cooperation programs to help other countries transform their institutions that could be applied to the reserve challenge in Taiwan. The Defense Institutional Reform Initiative (DIRI), run by OSD and the Naval Postgraduate School, and Military Defense Advisors (MoDA), run by the Defense Security Cooperation Agency, are two examples that could bring external assistance to help the Taiwan MND transform the reserves.

4. *Organize the reserves for the era of the all-volunteer force.* As part of the transition to a more strategically focused reserve force,

Taiwan authorities should consider a role for the reserves in providing technically specialized personnel and units to augment the active force. We discuss some of the recommended mission skills and specialized units later in this chapter, specific to the conduct of operations in key domains and geographic areas. These are not, however, the only potential areas where Taiwan could alleviate the demands placed on active personnel in low-density, high-value positions in the new threat environment. Reserve augmentation of pilots and information technology specialists, for example, would send a clear signal to Beijing that the Taiwan reserves would add considerable capability in mission critical areas. On Taiwan's part, however, this requires resources and policies that ensure augmentation from reservists with levels of professionalism and training that are indistinguishable from that of their active-duty counterparts. As we note in the appendix, where we briefly consider reserve reform efforts in other countries, expanding the reserve force to include women would provide a wider talent pool to fill specialist positions and units.

None of these proposed initiatives would reduce in any way the combat performance of the reserve force, and they may help improve it. By linking the reserve force with leadership statements, military exercises, arms sales, and other politically sensitive aspects of Taiwan's defense, Taipei might be able to confront Beijing decisionmakers with the reality that any invasion campaign they may consider undertaking would meet with overwhelming resistance, or at least greater resistance than planning calculations had surmised. This would portray an augmented role for the reserve force. In addition, the United States has a potentially decisive role in helping to shape that contribution.

Undermining PRC Advantages, Exploiting Key Domains and Geography

At the highest level, the competition between Taipei and Beijing is for political legitimacy. However, the essential question in the strategic balance is whether the PLA has the ability to project power across the Taiwan Strait, and whether or not Taiwan has the ability to defend against that invasion.

Several important domains effect how Taipei and Beijing judge the military balance in the Taiwan Strait. These are the electromagnetic, air, and sea domains. Both sides of the Strait perceive these three areas of competition to be foundational for successfully achieving or deterring an invasion. From the PLA's perspective, it not possible to launch amphibious operations against Taiwan without undisputed control over the electromagnetic, air, and sea domains. From the Taiwan military's perspective, seizing superiority in these domains at a time and place of its own choosing is critical for defending against invasion.

The contest for the electromagnetic, air, and sea domains would likely be concentrated in the first two phases of operations. The first phase of a notional PLA invasion would include blockade and strike operations on the PRC side, and force preservation efforts on the Taiwan side. The second phase would involve PLA forces crossing the Strait and inserting a sizable force onto Taiwan, which would confront Taiwan's joint combat operations. Both the PLA and the Taiwan military appear to view the first two phases of their operational plans to be the most dynamic. The third phase, the PLA's on-island fight versus Taiwan's homeland defense, would occur only after complete and favorable phase one and two outcomes set the conditions for the PLA invasion. This is something not usually taken for granted by planners on either side.[3]

Taiwan optimizes the reserve force to play a crucial role in the third and final phase of homeland defense operations. The reserve force has supporting roles to play in Taiwan's force preservation and joint

---

[3] This discussion draws from Ian Easton, *The Chinese Invasion Threat: Taiwan's Defense and American Strategy in Asia*, Arlington, Va.: Project 2049 Institute, forthcoming.

combat operations phases, but its principal role is to serve as a last line of defense. The drawback of the current approach is that it places the reserve force in a passive and reactive position. Opportunities may exist for building a future reserve force that can contribute more in phase one and phase two operations, with the objective of denying the PLA control over the electromagnetic, air, and sea domains. In this role, the reserve force could play a more proactive role earlier in conflict and help ensure that the initiative is not lost. To prepare the reserve forces for such a role, it is essential to consider how it could contribute in the likely geographic areas where a battle would ensue. Three areas are of particular importance: the PRC coastal area, the Taiwan Strait, and the coastal areas of Taiwan proper.

The first geographic battle space that presents itself is the PRC coastal area. This area comprises islands in the Taiwan Strait and littoral areas in the provinces of Fujian, Guangdong, and Zhejiang. The PLA would rely heavily on port facilities, airports, army aviation bases, and missile launch sites in the PRC coastal area to launch attacks on Taiwan. It would also rely on highways and railways to move its forces and their supplies. This infrastructure is all static and readily identifiable. Moreover, much of it depends on uninterrupted communications through tunnels, across mountain passes, and over bridges. Taiwan controls three island groups that are located close to the three major sea transport hubs on the PRC side of the Taiwan Strait.[4]

The second geographic battlespace that presents itself is the maritime areas around the Taiwan Strait. This consists of known sea lines that connect the mainland to Taiwan. As a general matter, any Chinese amphibious fleet or fleets would probably assemble at preplanned points near the mainland before sailing across the Taiwan Strait to anchorage areas off the coast of Taiwan. The PLA would select invasion routes with an eye toward reducing travel times across the Strait, because armadas at sea are large exposed targets vulnerable to attack. Selected invasion routes would also be influenced by PLA planning assumptions and information regarding sea depths, sea bottom conditions, weather conditions, minefield locations (both friendly and adver-

---

[4] Easton, forthcoming.

sary), and the location of Taiwan naval, air, and coastal defense assets. In addition, any PLA invasion fleet would want to avoid sailing within antiship missile range of offshore islands controlled by Taiwan.[5]

The third geographic battlespace that presents itself is the coastal areas of Taiwan proper. There are a very small number of potential PLA landing zones on Taiwan. An ideal landing zone would be a beach or river delta large enough to accommodate at least a battalion of amphibious forces. The beachhead would be located within a few miles of a large airfield and a small-to-medium-sized port facility that paratroopers or commandos could seize to serve as a point of entry for follow-on forces. The ideal landing zone would offer easy access to important tactical geography, such as transportation hubs and high plateaus overlooking major cities. From the PLA planning perspective, the closer to Taipei that large forces could land, the better.[6]

To position itself more effectively for a long-term strategic competition, Taiwan could consider future reserve force roles, missions, and capabilities to counter PRC capability advantages in projecting an invasion force across, over, above, and through the aforementioned geographic battlespaces. The most effective opportunities would be to bolster reserve force capabilities for phase one and phase two operations, especially those that can contribute to denying the PLA unimpeded access to the electromagnetic, air, and maritime domains. There are significant constraints to PLA amphibious operations inherent to the unique military geography of the Taiwan Strait area. Taiwan could better exploit this with a mix of reserve force investments targeted to take advantage of specific PLA vulnerabilities.

Electromagnetic Denial

Taiwan is at the forefront of information and communications technology (ICT) development and utilization, and a key link in the supply chain enabling the global proliferation of advanced electronics.[7]

---

[5] Easton, forthcoming.

[6] Easton, forthcoming.

[7] For example, see Tim Culpan, "Apple Opens Secret Laboratory in Taiwan to Develop New Screens," *Bloomberg*, December 14, 2015; Chung Jung-feng and Christie Chen, "Taiwan

Because of its progress, communications traffic saturates Taiwan's airwaves, giving it unique experience and ability in the area of frequency spectrum management.[8] It is not clear whether the Taiwan reserve force fully exploits the considerable technological expertise and professional talents of the reservists who work day-to-day in the commercial ICT sector. By assisting the active-duty force in denying the PLA control over the electromagnetic spectrum early in a conflict, reserve units could degrade adversary air and maritime combat effects and contribute to the disruption of their operational plans.

To take advantage of the ICT capabilities resident in the reserve forces, we recommend that the Reserve Command form special reserve units composed of ICT experts for electronic and cyber warfare. Notional electronic and cyber warfare reserve units could organize for and undertake missions including computer network defense, computer network attack, and computer network exploitation, in addition to traditional jamming and counter-jamming missions. These units could contribute to the protection of Taiwan's military communications and sensor networks, while also providing advanced capabilities for disabling adversary networks and collecting intelligence. In addition, they could augment Taiwan's existing capabilities for jamming PLA radars, radios, satellites, drones, and missiles. To maximize effectiveness, reserve electronic warfare units would likely require frequent and nontraditional training to keep their specialized skills fresh and up to date.

Air Denial

Taiwan has an array of modern air defense capabilities for layered protection of its airspace against the full spectrum of PLA air and missile threats. This defense network includes long-range air and missile defense units deployed on Taiwan's frontline islands at locations that

---

Wins Most Gold Medals at Asia Pacific ICT Competition," *Focus Taiwan*, November 26, 2015; and John Liu, "US, Local Officials Stress ICT at COMPUTEX," *China Times*, June 3, 2015.

[8] Mark A. Stokes, *Revolutionizing Taiwan's Security: Leveraging C4ISR for Traditional and Nontraditional Challenges*, Arlington, Va.: Project 2049 Institute, September 2009, pp. 26–27.

allow extensive coverage over PRC airbases. The Penghu Islands serve as a secondary air and missile defense outpost for covering approaches across the Taiwan Strait. On Taiwan, there are large numbers of point defenses for intercepting aerial intruders that might target critical ROC military facilities and civilian infrastructure early in a conflict to paralyze the island's military forces. However, modern missile systems offer considerable ability to penetrate defensive screens through the application of multi-directional saturation attacks. The PLA has the world's largest and most sophisticated arsenal of theater missiles, and its capacity for threatening Taiwan with air and missile strikes continues to grow.

In August 2014, Taiwan announced its intention to invest $2.5 billion into the large-scale production of a new indigenous air and missile defense system, the TIEN KUNG III, to replace aging HAWK units.[9] Taiwan is also taking the delivery of the last of ten PATRIOT PAC-3 fire units and integrating them into units that previously operated HAWK batteries. Reportedly, manpower shortages in air defense units may result in the early retirement of still-serviceable missiles.[10]

To fill this gap, we recommend that the Reserve Command form special reserve units to maintain and operate legacy air defense missiles, such as HAWK, to bolster Taiwan's ability to deny the PLA air superiority in a high-intensity conflict of extended duration. In addition, Taiwan could train and equip special reserve force units with short-range air defense missiles, such as STINGER. Working in tandem with active-duty units, reserve force air defense teams on Taiwan and offshore islands could assist in denying enemy aircraft unimpeded access to the airspace above the Taiwan Strait, greatly complicating the PLA's ability to project power. To maximize effectiveness, however, these reserve air defense units would likely require more frequent and concentrated refresher training than is currently offered to reservists in the five to seven days of such training required in a two-year period.

---

[9] "Taiwan to Spend $2.5 Billion on Anti-Missile Systems," AFP Taipei, August 30, 2014.

[10] Authors' discussions with Taiwan defense experts with direct access on August 4, 2015, in Arlington, Va., and on October 4–6, 2015, in Williamsburg, Va.

Sea Denial

Taiwan is developing a robust reconnaissance-strike network for defending its coastline against approaching PLA invasion fleets.[11] This network centers on advanced antiship missiles launched from submarines, surface ships, aircraft, coastal bunkers, and road-mobile launch vehicles. Any hypothetical counter-amphibious operation would logically begin with missile strikes on enemy transport ships at embarkation points along the PRC coast. Strikes would also focus on the PLA's offshore fleet assembly zones and anchorage sites near Taiwan.[12] In addition to missile strikes, the Taiwan Navy would conduct mine warfare against the PLA Navy to deny access to potential invasion routes across the Strait. Mobilized naval reserve units would play an important role in operating vessels engaged in laying minefields.[13] Reservists and contractors would further assist in the deployment of obstacles and defense works at potential landing sites along the Taiwan coastline.[14]

The PRC's naval modernization program is on track to improve Chinese amphibious lift and cross-Strait power-projection capabilities in the years ahead.[15] Fleet air defenses will offer greater protection for amphibious assault and troop transport ships. At the same time, the PLA Navy's large and growing fleets of submarines, destroyers, unmanned aerial vehicles, and maritime strike aircraft are likely to constrain Taiwan's ability to conduct effective naval operations to counter invasion armadas.[16] To adapt to this challenging maritime defense environment, Taiwan could consider deploying a much larger force of missiles and

---

[11] Ian Easton, *Taiwan's Naval Role in the Rebalance to Asia*, Arlington, Va.: Project 2049 Institute, March 2015, pp. 4–5.

[12] Easton, 2015, pp. 4–5.

[13] Authors' discussions with Taiwanese military authority on October 5, 2015, in Williamsburg, Va.

[14] Liu Jian, 2004, p. 30.

[15] See Ronald O'Rourke, *China Naval Modernization: Implications for U.S. Navy Capabilities*, Washington, D.C.: Congressional Research Service, July 28, 2015, pp. 34–35; and Yang You-hung, 2013, p. 103.

[16] See Office of Naval Intelligence, *The PLA Navy: New Capabilities and Missions for the 21st Century*, Washington, D.C., 2015, pp. 13–23.

mines. The reserve force could provide the extra labor necessary to maintain and operate this expanded force. Enabling capabilities could include next-generation unmanned systems equipped with advanced sensors for maritime domain awareness in support of antiship missile and mine warfare units.

Therefore, we recommend that the Reserve Command form special reserve units for operations employing antiship missiles and expanded mine warfare capabilities, and unmanned surveillance systems. In addition to developing specialist units for operating unmanned surveillance systems, the reserve force could expand units specializing in antisubmarine warfare missions. Assuming sufficient resources dedicated to specialized reserve units for meeting their training and equipment needs, Taiwan could field a much larger and more lethal sea denial force for countering the PRC's naval buildup.

CHAPTER SEVEN

Conclusion

This report has provided an overview of how Taiwan's reserve force is structured and described its roles, missions, capabilities, and challenges. We have also assessed the Taiwan reserve force role in cross-Strait competition and made recommendations for future Taiwan reserve force roles, missions, and capabilities, based on the requirement to counter PRC advantages in air and maritime power-projection capabilities. As part of this effort, we have identified potential enabling capabilities and specialist units that Taiwan could incorporate into its reserve force structure, which would not only expand reserve force capabilities but also raise its strategic profile in deterring PRC military action.

We list our concluding recommendations in three categories, as follows:

1. Employ the reserve force as an instrument of statecraft for deterring PRC use of force and other forms of coercion. New initiatives along this line of effort might include:
    -   Publicly highlight the reserve force in leadership statements, published defense strategy documents, and the Taiwan press. As an example, recent reporting notes moves to correct administrative shortcomings in call-up training.[1]
    -   Highlight the reserve force at Taiwan's annual HAN KUANG exercises. Mobilizing multiple reserve brigades during the annual HAN KUANG exercises and integrating them into

---

[1] Joseph Yeh, "Defense Ministry Amends Reservist Call-Up Loophole," *China Post*, April 22, 2016.

live-fire events with active-duty units likely would be an effective initiative in this regard.

- Engage in military-to-military exchanges with the U.S. Department of Defense, including OSD, the Joint Staff, and the U.S. Army, that directly relate to improving the reserve force. Considerations could include establishment of a joint reserve force working group, led on the U.S. side by the Office of the Assistant Secretary of Defense for Manpower and Reserve Affairs, and regular visits to the United States by senior leaders of Taiwan's Reserve Command. Taiwan may also consider sending reservists to the United States for professional military education and technical training.

- Organize the reserves in keeping with plans for the era of the all-volunteer force. As part of the transition to a more strategically focused reserve force, Taiwan authorities should consider a role for the reserves in providing technically specialized personnel and units to augment the active force. Reserve augmentation of pilots and information technology specialists, for example, would send a clear signal to Beijing that the Taiwan reserves would add considerable capability in mission critical areas.

2. Consider how the reserve force can undermine PRC advantages in the initial stages of an invasion scenario, and better exploit domain-specific and geographic aspects of the conflict. New concepts along this line might include the following:

- Exploring how the reserve force can contribute more during phase one and phase two operations (force preservation and joint combat) so that Taiwan does not cede the strategic initiative to the PRC at the outset of conflict.

- Considering where the reserve force can better exploit the favorable geography of the Taiwan Strait battle space to target critical PLA vulnerabilities in projecting power.

3. Develop future reserve roles, missions, and capabilities, including specialist units and specialist jobs to incorporate into the reserve force structure, to exploit enabling capabilities, and pro-

vide additional equipment and training resources to support these units. Three particularly promising areas are:

- Constraining access to the electromagnetic domain by forming special reserve units composed of ICT experts for electronic and cyber warfare.
- Denying unimpeded access to the air domain by forming special reserve units for maintaining and operating large numbers of air defense missiles.
- Impeding access to the sea domain by forming special reserve units for operations employing antiship missiles, expanded mine warfare capabilities, advanced antisubmarine warfare technologies, and unmanned surveillance systems.

To reinforce and realize the advantages from the recommendations above, Taiwan must develop and resource new training programs. Current reserve force training is insufficient to meet the challenges posed by the increasing threat from the PLA. To be effective, the units and personnel focused on the new areas we recommend must be indistinguishable from their counterparts in the regular force, allowing them to bring their special skills to bear quickly during wartime operations. It is imperative that specialist reservists spend significant quantities of time (at least two or three weeks) every year engaged in intense and realistic training. This requires the government of Taiwan to increase funding allotted for training, education, and personnel development.

The current funding provided to the reserve force is inadequate to meet the demands imposed by the volunteer force transition and the PRC's rapid military buildup. We recommend that Taiwan's Legislative Yuan increase the reserve force budget on top of the existing defense mark. We further recommend that the Executive Yuan make building a strong national reserve force one of its top priorities. The long-term survival of Taiwan's democracy in the face of possible PRC invasion depends on perfecting capabilities for all-out defense. It is beyond the scope of this study to assess optimum approaches to developing, funding, and executing a new training regimen, but such a consideration is necessary if Taiwan's leaders expect the reserve force to reinforce cross-Strait deterrence, and defend Taiwan should deterrence fail.

Constraints on Taiwan's defense budget and competition for resources are pushing the MND to consider more innovative employment of its military force to meet the growing threat from mainland China. One area of interest, explored in this study, is how Taiwan can use reserve forces more effectively against that threat. Based on our analysis, there are many opportunities for reserve forces to play a significant role in undermining potential PRC military force projection capabilities, and for deterring PRC attack by becoming more conspicuously capable in specific domains and mission areas. We have offered recommendations specifying what we believe to be the most promising areas in this regard, and pointed to areas where further study and analysis could lead to enhanced Taiwan reserve force readiness and effectiveness.

Case Studies of Possible Lessons from Other Reserve Forces

To glean potential lessons for Taiwan reserve force transformation from the reserve forces of other countries, we briefly reviewed the reserve forces of Finland, Singapore, Japan, and Georgia. We find that Finland and Singapore offer some valuable lessons. Japan does as well, although to a lesser extent, but Georgia offers little in the way of positive lessons for Taiwan's future reserve force development. We highlight some of the key lessons here and, in the remainder of this appendix, discuss each case in further detail.

Finland

As of 2015, Finland has 354,000 reservists and 22,000 active personnel in the Finnish Defence Forces. Most of the reserves, 285,000, are in the Army; 31,000 are in the Navy; and the remaining 38,000 are in the Air Force. Apart from its 2,800 regular paramilitary forces, Finland has 11,500 paramilitary reserves. These figures indicate a high level of reliance on the reserve force in case of conflicts and crises. In terms of training, 25,000 reservists per year do refresher training, with a total obligation of 40 days (75 for NCOs and 100 for officers) between conscript service and age 50 (age 60 for NCOs and officers).[1]

---

[1] International Institute for Strategic Studies, 2015, "Chapter Four: Europe," p. 88.

Reform Efforts

As the *Armed Forces Journal* has noted,

> Finnish defense forces carry out a broad range of defense and
> civil support activities . . . including forest firefighting, search
> and rescue, and explosive ordnance disposal. They may also sup-
> plement law enforcement organization. These executive assis-
> tance tasks, as they are known in Finland remain quite common.
> Nearly all of them are carried out by conscripts on active duty
> who will soon become part of the reserve force structure.[2]

Since 2011, the Finnish government has made efforts to reform
the Finnish Defence Forces. The Finnish Defence Forces' 2011 annual
report, for example, emphasized reforming the conscription system,
which forms the basis of the reserve system.[3] Reforms continued apace
in 2012, although the annual report of that year listed tying the reserve
and voluntary national defense to planning and implementation as
an unresolved issue.[4] According to the Ministry of Defence's annual
report, Finland completed implementation of defense reform in 2014.
This led to an overall reorganization, an increase in the number of days
spent in the field, and an increase in the number of live-fire and combat
exercises.[5] At the time, the reforms gave the Defence Forces wartime
strength of just over 4 percent of the population.[6]

Other reforms include increasing opportunities to train and gain
experience and incentives to motivate reservists. In September 2014,
for instance, the Defence Forces announced plans to increase reserve
refresher training.[7] In 2015, Finland sent a unit composed mainly of

---

[2] "Send in the Reserves," *Armed Forces Journal*, February 1, 2012.

[3] Finnish Defence Forces, *Annual Report 2011*, 2012.

[4] Finnish Defence Forces, *Annual Report 2012*, 2013.

[5] Finnish Defence Forces, *Annual Report 2014*, 2014.

[6] Finnish Defence Forces, 2014.

[7] "Defence Forces Plans Increase in Refresher Training," *Finland Times*, September 24, 2014.

reservists (270 out of a 290-person unit) to the NATO Response Force.[8] Also in November 2015, Defence Minister Jussi Niinistö announced a shortening of the notice period for inviting conscripts to refresher courses while also proposing the idea of using them more widely in standby duties.[9] Finally, according to the *Finland Times*, local forces are to be created within the army, and within these local forces, reservists "will have the opportunity to rise to the highest ranks in the leadership positions."[10] These local forces are themselves composed largely of reservists.

Although the Finnish government has denied such claims, there is little doubt that Finland undertook these reforms with Russia in mind. Relations between the two countries are increasingly tense, and, in 2015, the Finnish government sent letters to reservists, setting out their roles "in the event of war."[11]

Singapore

As of 2015, Singapore has 312,500 reservists and 72,500 active personnel. Most of the reserves are concentrated in the Army (300,000). The Navy has 5,000 reservists, while the Air Force has 7,500 reservists. There are also 44,000 paramilitary reservists and 75,100 active paramilitary personnel.[12] As with Finland, these figures indicate a high level of reliance on the reserve force in case of conflicts and crises. Conscripts serve two years in the Full-Time National Service.[13] Afterward, there is annual training until the age of 50 for officers and until

---

[8] "Finland to Contribute in NATO Response Force Readiness," *Finland Times*, November 4, 2014.

[9] "Defence Minister for Shortening Notice Period," *Finland Times*, November 10, 2015.

[10] "Local Forces to Be Formed Under Defence Reforms," *Finland Times*, April 29, 2014.

[11] Nick Squires, "Finland Tells 900,000 Reservists Their Roles 'In the Event of War,'" *The Telegraph*, May 21, 2015.

[12] International Institute for Strategic Studies, 2015, "Chapter Six: Asia," p. 283.

[13] Ministry of Defence of Singapore, "NS Matters: About Us," web page, last updated on January 15, 2016.

the age of 40 for other army ranks.[14] Such annual training, known as Operationally Ready National Service, may go up to a maximum of 40 days.[15] Reservists are also known as Operationally Ready National Servicemen.[16]

Reserve Force Reforms

Singapore established its National Service in 1967. The government began undertaking reform of the system in March 2013, when it set up the Committee to Strengthen National Service (CSNS). Leading CSNS's work was a steering committee, chaired by Minister of Defence Ng Eng Hen and composed of 19 additional members.[17] CSNS completed its work in March 2014. In the process, it gathered feedback from more than 40,000 members of the public.[18] During this period, members of the steering committee also took study trips to Finland and Switzerland to understand the conscription systems of these countries.[19]

Ultimately, the committee came up with a list of 30 recommendations divided into six categories, all of which the Singaporean government subsequently accepted. These include (1) creating a strong National Service training system, (2) more opportunities for National Servicemen to contribute, (3) creating a Singapore Armed Forces Volunteer Corps (SAFVC), (4) increasing recognition and benefits for National Servicemen, (5) expanding community support for National

---

[14] International Institute for Strategic Studies, 2015, "Chapter Six: Asia," p. 283.

[15] Ministry of Defence of Singapore, "NS Matters: For NSmen," web page, last updated on October 29, 2014d.

[16] Ministry of Defence of Singapore, "Factsheet: Reservist on Voluntary Extended Reserve Service (ROVERS) Scheme," last updated on May 12, 2015.

[17] Ministry of Defence of Singapore, "Strengthening NS: The Committee," 2014a; Ministry of Defence of Singapore, "Fact Sheet: Committee to Strengthen National Service," May 8, 2013.

[18] Ministry of Defence of Singapore, "Strengthen National Service," last updated on May 22, 2014.

[19] Lim Wee Kiak, "Bringing National Service Up to Date," *The Straits Times*, June 25, 2014.

Servicemen, and (6) easing administrative restrictions in order to create a positive National Service experience.[20]

Among these reforms, the creation of the SAFVC is particularly notable in that it "[enables] women, new citizens and first generation Permanent Residents to contribute to national defence."[21] This is a timely reform, as outside observers have noted the shrinking pool of enlistees for conscription due to Singapore's declining birthrate. Indeed, *The Straits Times* has projected that the number of enlistees will fall to 19,500 by 2025, compared with 26,000 in 2011.[22] Meanwhile, other reforms increase the monetary incentives for enlistees. While National Service remains compulsory, these reforms help to make it more attractive and less of an imposition on the public.

Japan

As of 2015, Japan has 56,100 reservists and 247,150 active members in its Self-Defense Force (SDF). The vast majority of the reservists belong to the Ground Self-Defense Force (GSDF): 46,000 are in the General Reserve Army and another 8,200 are in the Ready Reserve Army. The Maritime Self-Defense Force (MSDF) has another 1,100, and the Air Self-Defense Force (ASDF) has the remaining 800.[23]

Evolution of the SDF Reserve Forces

The state of the SDF reserve force has historically been poor. Edward Olsen in 1985 described the reserves of the GSDF as being "sizeable" but also "poorly run and under few obligations to respond to a call-up.

---

[20] Ministry of Defence of Singapore, "Recommendations by the Committee to Strengthen National Service," last updated on June 10, 2014c.

[21] Ministry of Defence of Singapore, 2014a.

[22] Ong Hwee Hwee, "Budget Backgrounder: National Service," *The Straits Times*, March 6, 2014.

[23] International Institute for Strategic Studies, 2015, "Chapter Six: Asia," p. 257.

The ASDF and MSDF reserves are scarcely worthy of the name."[24] In 1994, Thomas Wilborn wrote that SDF lacked an adequate reserve system and that the reserves, the majority belonging to the GSDF, received very limited training and poor compensation.[25]

Beginning in 1995, the Japanese government began an attempt to reform the SDF, including its much criticized reserve system, by authorizing the National Defense Program Outline.[26] As described in the outline, Japan introduced the system of SDF Ready Reserve Personnel in 1998.[27] Later, in 2001, Japan created the Candidates for SDF Reserve Personnel system, which recruits volunteer applicants with no previous experience as uniformed SDF personnel. The goal of the system is to "make good use of civilian expertise from the perspective of increasing opportunities for people's contact with the SDF and cultivating and expanding a foundation for national defense."[28]

As a result of these changes, the SDF now has three parallel reserve systems—the SDF Ready Reserve Personnel, the SDF Reserve Personnel, and the Candidate for SDF Reserve Personnel. These three parallel systems are meant to supplement SDF Regular Personnel, whose numbers are normally "kept to the minimum needed to respond to situations."[29] Table A.1 provides an overview of the three systems.

In spite these reforms, the SDF Reserves have continued to perform poorly. This was evident in the response to the 2011 Tohoku earthquake and tsunami, during which the Ministry of Defense activated the reservists for the very first time since the system's creation in

---

[24] Edward A. Olsen, *U.S.-Japan Strategic Reciprocity: A Neo-Internationalist View*, 1985, p. 84.

[25] Thomas L. Wilborn, *Japan's Self-Defense Forces: What Dangers to Northeast Asia?* Strategic Studies Institute, U.S. Army War College, May 1, 1994, p. 21.

[26] Tetsushi Kajimoto, "GSDF Ready Reservists Sworn in," *The Japan Times*, April 27, 1998.

[27] Ministry of Defense of Japan, *Defense of Japan 2006*, "Defense Chronology," p. 569.

[28] Ministry of Defense of Japan, *Defense of Japan 2005*, "Chapter 5: People and the Defense Agency/SDF," p. 74.

[29] Ministry of Defense of Japan, *Defense of Japan 2007*, "Chapter 4: Citizens of Japan, the Ministry of Defense and the SDF," p. 403.

Table A.1
Overview of Systems Related to SDF Reserve Personnel

	SDF Reserve Personnel	SDF Ready Reserve Personnel	Candidate for SDF Reserve Personnel
Basic concept	When defense call-up or disaster call-up is received, they serve as SDF Regular Personnel	When defense call-up is received, or under similar conditions, they serve as SDF Regular Personnel in a predetermined GSDF unit, as part of the basic framework of defense capability	Appointed as SDF Reserve Personnel upon completion of education and training
Candidate	Former Regular Personnel, former SDF Ready Reserve Personnel, former Reserve Personnel	Former Regular Personnel, former Reserve Personnel	(Same for General and Technical) Inexperienced SDF Personnel (includes those with less than a year of SDF experience)
Age	Enlisted (Lower): 18–36 years old Officer, Warrant Officer, Enlisted (Upper): Under two years above the retirement age	Enlisted (Lower): 18–31 years old Officer, Warrant Officer, Enlisted (Upper): Under three years below the retirement age for each rank	General: over 18 and under 34 years old Technical: over 53 and under 55 years old depending on technical skills possessed after the age of 18
Employment	Employment on screening, based on application Candidate for SDF Reserve Personnel is appointed as SDF Reserve Personnel upon completion of education and training	Employment on screening, based on application	General: Employment on examination, based on application Technical: Employment on screening, based on application

Table A.1—continued

	SDF Reserve Personnel	SDF Ready Reserve Personnel	Candidate for SDF Reserve Personnel
Rank	Former Regular Personnel: As a rule, rank at the point of retirement SDF Ready Reserve Personnel: Current specified rank Former Reserve Personnel and Former Ready Reserve Personnel: As a rule, rank at the point of retirement Candidate for Reserve Personnel General: Private Technical: Assignment based on skills	Former Regular Personnel: As a rule, rank at the point of retirement Former Reserve Personnel: As a rule, designated rank at the point of retirement	Not designated
Term of service	Three years/one term	Three years/one term	General: Maximum of three years Technical: Maximum of two years
Education/ Training	Although the Self-Defense Forces Law designates a maximum of 20 days per year, actual implementation is a minimum of 5 days per year	30 days per year	General: 50 days within a maximum of three years (equivalent to SDF personnel cadet course) Technical: 10 days within a maximum of two years (training to serve as an SDF Regular Personnel by utilizing each skill)
Promotion	Promotion is determined by screening the service record of personnel who have fulfilled the service term (actual serving days)	Promotion is determined by screening the service record of personnel who have fulfilled the service term (actual serving days)	Since there is no designated rank, there is no promotion

Table A.1—continued

	SDF Reserve Personnel	SDF Ready Reserve Personnel	Candidate for SDF Reserve Personnel
Benefits, allowances, and other terms	Training Call-Up Allowance: ¥8,100/day SDF Reserve Allowance: ¥4,000/month	Training Call-Up Allowance: ¥10,400–14,200/day SDF Ready Reserve Allowance: ¥16,000/month Continuous Service Incentive Allowance: ¥120,000/one term Special subsidy for corporations employing Ready Reserve Personnel: ¥42,500/month	Education and Training Call-up Allowance: ¥7,900/day Allowance as candidate for SDF Reserve Personnel is not paid because defense call-up duty is not imposed on them
Call-up duty and other duties	Defense call-up, civil protection call-up, disaster call-up, training call-up	Defense call-up, civil protection call-up, security call-up, disaster call-up, training call-up	Education and training call-up

SOURCE: Adapted from Ministry of Defense of Japan, *Defense of Japan 2015*, 2015a, p. 251.

1954.[30] The Finance Ministry's annual inspection report was particularly damning: "Only 17 percent of reserves said they were available for duty after the March 2011 calamities, with 0.3 percent mobilized. . . . The program had a budget of ¥8 billion for the year through March 2012."[31]

More recently, in 2014, a senior military official noted, "The number of civilians registered as reservists . . . is dwindling, mainly due to the difficulty of balancing training with civilian careers." Additionally, "although the Defense Ministry aims to recruit 47,900 reserves, only about 70 percent of the positions have been filled, while the number of vacant posts is increasing year by year."[32] To reverse this trend, the

---

[30] Yuki Tatsumi, *Great Eastern Japan Earthquake: "Lessons Learned" for Japanese Defense Policy*," Stimson Center, November 2012, p. 12.

[31] "Azumi Blasts 'Wasteful' SDF Reserves," *The Japan Times*, July 5, 2012.

[32] "SDF Struggling to Attract Enough Reservists," *The Japan Times*, August 19, 2014.

Ministry of Defense has attempted to offer certain incentives to businesses that employ reservists. In its 2016 budget request, for example, it stated that it "will request corporation tax reductions of ¥400,000 per an increased number of employees (SDF reserve personnel, etc.) for business owners/employers that satisfy certain requirements."[33]

Georgia

There are few reliable sources on the current number of reservists in the Georgian Armed Forces. However, several sources—again, of uncertain reliability—note that Georgia had 140,000 reservists as of 2014[34] and 20,650 active personnel in 2015.[35] The International Institute for Strategic Studies' *The Military Balance* gives no information regarding the total number of reserves in the Georgian Armed Forces, noting only the number of active personnel. However, the 2015 edition does indicate that there is a conscript liability of 18 months. Presumably, Georgia may call persons who have fulfilled this liability into action in times of conflict or crisis, thereby serving as a *de facto* reserve force. For reference, in 2015 the number of conscripts per service branch was as follows: 3,750 for the Army, 300 for the Air Force, and 1,600 active reservists for the National Guard under the operational control of the Army, for 5,650 conscripts.[36]

Reform Efforts and Results

Beginning in the early 2000s, the Georgian government attempted to expand the number of reservists dramatically. Initially, it planned

[33] Ministry of Defense of Japan, "Defense Programs and Budget of Japan: Overview of FY2016 Budget Request," August 2015, p. 32.

[34] Annyssa Bellal, ed., *The War Report: Armed Conflict in 2014*, Oxford, UK: Oxford University Press, 2015, p. 88; "Republic of Georgia, Background Brief: CENEX 2013," University of Denver Josef Korbel School of International Studies, Crisis Engagement and Negotiation Exercise (CENEX) 2013, p. 2.

[35] International Institute for Strategic Studies, 2015, "Chapter Five: Russia and Eurasia," p. 179.

[36] International Institute for Strategic Studies, 2015, pp. 179–180.

to train 15,000–20,000 reservists by the end of 2005, which it later expanded to 100,000 by 2012.[37] However, even at that time, critics complained that this plan was overly ambitious, notably regarding the inadequately short three-week training period.[38]

The shortcomings of this plan became readily apparent during the 2008 war with Russia: "The reservists received only 18–24 days of basic training, which led to disastrous results after 10,000 were dispatched to defend Gori."[39] According to a Russian intelligence source, "Georgia suffered such heavy losses [of up to 3,000 servicemen and police during the South Ossetia conflict] because of the poor training and low morale of its military personnel, especially reservists."[40] This situation appears to persist even as of 2015. Georgian Defense Minister Tina Khidasheli reportedly said, "Very few conscripts go through proper military training, comprising no more than 10% of total military personnel. Rather than readying for future combats or jobs, the remaining 90% are employed as free (unqualified) labor to guard Georgian prisons, military bases and government buildings."[41]

According to Nodar Kharshiladze, the former deputy prime minister who personally oversaw the establishment of the military reserve system, none of the previous models for structuring the reserves succeeded because the reserves themselves were politicized and used as such.[42]

The Georgian government has made concerted efforts at reform since the disastrous performance of the reserve force in 2008. In 2014,

[37] Liz Fuller and Richard Giragosian, "Georgia: What Is Behind Expansion of Armed Forces?" Radio Free Europe/Radio Liberty, September 19, 2007.

[38] Fuller and Giragosian, 2007.

[39] Stephen Jones, *Georgia: A Political History Since Independence*, New York: I.B. Tauris & Co. Ltd., 2013, p. 242.

[40] "Georgia Lost Up to 3,000 Men in S. Ossetia Conflict—Russian Source," *The Financial*, September 14, 2008.

[41] Eric Livny, "On Education and the Sacred Duty of Defending One's Motherland," *The Financial*, November 30, 2015.

[42] Giorgi Menabde, "Georgia Reviews Results of Its Military Reforms," *Eurasia Daily Monitor*, Vol. 11, No. 21, February 4, 2014.

the Ministry of Defense finished elaborating the draft document on the GAF Reserve and Mobilization System.[43] The 2014 National Military Strategy also stressed the importance of developing a "reserve and mobilization system considering existing threats, available forces and limited resources available to ensure the country's defence."[44] The National Security Concept, meanwhile, states, "it is a priority to cooperate with partner countries and to learn from their experience. . . . Therefore, the increased interoperability of the Georgian Armed Forces with NATO remains the priority of Georgian defense reform."[45]

To that end, Georgia sought assistance from NATO's National Reserve Forces Committee, which it initially joined as an observer in November 2013.[46] In April 2014, it attended the Committee Staff Officers assembly in France. In October 2015, it hosted a working conference of the Committee ahead of an extended meeting held in February 2016 in Brussels.[47]

Conclusion

Qualitative and Quantitative Changes to Training

One of the noted problems with Taiwan's reserve system is the limited and ineffective training that reservists receive. Conscripts report for duty only once every two years for a mere five to seven days of refresher training. This is less than Japan's system, in which reserve personnel complete a minimum of five days of training each year. In the run-up to the 2008 war with Russia, Georgian reservists also had short and poor quality training, which ultimately led to extremely poor performance.

---

[43] Ministry of Defence of Georgia, *White Book 2014*, 2014, p. 11.

[44] Ministry of Defence of Georgia, *National Military Strategy*, 2014, p. 9.

[45] Ministry of Foreign Affairs of Georgia, *National Security Concept of Georgia*, no date, p. 15.

[46] "A Working Conference of National Reserve Forces Committee," *Newsday Georgia*, October 23, 2015.

[47] "A Working Conference of National Reserve Force Committee," 2015.

By comparison, Singapore and Finland reserves have annual training of up to 40 days, and even more for personnel that are more senior. Training that is more frequent would be one possible reform of the Taiwan reserve system. Better-quality and more realistic training—such as the types of live-fire and combat exercises conducted in Finland—would also be beneficial to improving the reserve force's combat readiness.

Diversified Duties

In addition to improvements in training, Taiwan's reserve force might also benefit from more diversified employment. Finnish forces carry out a broad range of defense and civil support activities and are not limited to combat roles. Japan's SDF reserve personnel also train to respond to natural disasters. Singapore's National Service, meanwhile, is largely limited to military roles. However, Parag Khanna at the Lee Kuan Yew School of Public Policy has suggested that Singapore's National Service expand to include service in other sectors.[48] Taiwan could draw on all of these examples and employ its reserve force in ways that it traditionally has not. Using the reserve force in a wider range of activities may help reservists develop a broader range of skills and help the reserve force as a whole become more integrated into and attractive to Taiwan society. Mandatory national service requirements could include ministries other than the Ministry of Defense. National service could fill certain civil defense roles without further burdening the defense budget.

Expanding the Reserve Force

As pointed out earlier in this report, Taiwan is one of the world's rapidly "graying" societies. As such, it might benefit from the inclusion of women into the reserve force, as Singapore and other counties do. The Singapore Armed Forces Volunteer Corps allows women, new citizens, and first-generation permanent residents to contribute to the national defense in noncombat roles.

---

[48] Parag Khanna, "National Service for the 21st Century," *The Straits Times*, April 26, 2014.

Funding

This study also noted the Taiwan legislature's reluctance to increase defense spending as a factor hampering the effectiveness of Taiwan's military, including its reserve forces. Other countries have acknowledged the relationship between investment and force effectiveness as well. For instance, one of Singapore's reforms has focused on increasing monetary rewards to National Servicemen. Increased defense spending could contribute to the successful reform of Taiwan's reserve system, but increased spending alone may not be sufficient. In the case of Japan, a budget of ¥8 billion did little to improve the performance of SDF reserve personnel. Taiwan must allocate and target more of the defense budget (whether increased or static) to areas where improvements can yield greater force effectiveness—such as improving the quality and quantity of reserve force training.

International Cooperation

Finland and Georgia have benefited from increased international cooperation, principally with NATO. Indeed, Georgia has prioritized international cooperation in order to learn from the best practices of other countries. However, this option is not available to Taiwan. There is some possibility of increased cooperation with the United States, as recommended earlier in this report, but Washington may limit the extent of U.S.-Taiwan cooperation in order to avoid antagonizing China. Taiwan's regional neighbors will be even less likely to offer help.

Other Sources of Inspiration

Finally, in managing the reform of its reserve force, Taiwan may benefit from examining other examples than those covered in this limited survey. Switzerland and Israel are of particular interest. In the case of the former, members of the steering committee of Singapore's Committee to Strengthen National Service (CSNS) actually undertook study trips to both Finland and Switzerland while still formulating their proposals for how best to reform Singapore's National Service, and they found Switzerland's system a particularly helpful model. Switzerland's militia system focuses completely on rapid mobilization for homeland defense, and it has a conscription system for part-time service by all males under 50 and a voluntary system for women.

Israel presents a special case, and Taiwan may benefit even more from its example. Both countries face threat environments that are similar in one key respect: They confront an overtly hostile neighbor (in Taiwan's case) or neighbors (in Israel's) who pose an existential threat. Moreover, responding to these threats will likely require mobilization of conventional forces and, by extension, reserve forces.

There are similarities, of course, with Georgia. Russia is overtly hostile and also poses an existential threat to Georgia—to which both Abkhazia and South Ossetia serve as reminders. However, whereas Georgia's mobilization of both the active and reserve components of its armed forces in 2008 proved to be a disaster, Israel has had a better record of accomplishment. The Israeli Defense Forces have had both actual combat experience and more successes. In addition, Israel's reserve force is composed of both men and women, something that may be of interest to Taiwan given its shrinking pool of potential applicants.[49] For these reasons, it may be worthwhile for U.S. and Taiwan policymakers to study the Israeli system more closely.

Our bottom-line recommendations for consideration by Taiwan leaders, based on this admittedly limited survey of other reserve forces but reinforced by the analysis in the main body of this report, are that Taiwan should

- **invest more time and money into reserve force training**
- **further diversify reserve force missions and consider expanding roles for volunteers under a larger national service structure**
- **incorporate women into the force.**

Conversations with defense experts in Taiwan suggest that they have great respect for Singapore's reserve system, in particular, and view it as a strong model to follow. Israel is also a respected model, but

---

[49] International Institute for Strategic Studies, 2015, "Chapter Seven: Middle East and North Africa," p. 332.

Taipei is highly reluctant to have weapons in the homes of active-duty troops and reservists. Taiwan has extremely strict gun control rules, which have helped to curtail the three related threats of gangs, violent crime, and subversion (fifth-column activities).

Lists of Figures and Tables

Figures

Table

Abbreviations

ASDF	Air Self-Defense Force
CCP	Chinese Communist Party
CSNS	Committee to Strengthening National Service
GSDF	Ground Self-Defense Force
ICT	information and communications technology
MND	Ministry of National Defense
MSDF	Maritime Self-Defense Force
NATO	North Atlantic Treaty Organization
NCO	noncommissioned officer
NSmen	Operationally Ready National Servicemen
OSD	Office of the Secretary of Defense
PLA	People's Liberation Army
PRC	People's Republic of China
ROC	Republic of China
SAFVC	Singapore Armed Forces Volunteer Corps
SDF	Self-Defense Force

References

"2014 Spring Festival Combat Patrol: Tough Tri-Service Readiness Drills Held [2014春節戰鬥巡弋陸海空三軍精實戰力呈現]," *Defence International* [全球防衛雜誌]," No. 354, February 2014.

"All Volunteer Military Plans Postponed," *Taipei Times,* August 27, 2015.

"Armed Forces: Taiwan," *Jane's Sentinel Security Assessment: China and Northeast Asia*, September 28, 2015.

"Azumi Blasts 'Wasteful' SDF Reserves," *The Japan Times*, July 5, 2012. As of October 27, 2016:
http://www.japantimes.co.jp/news/2012/07/05/news/azumi-blasts-wasteful-sdf-reserves/#.Vo_OgpMrL1y

Bai Chun and Wu Junxi, "Overview of Taiwan Military Situation in 2013 [2013年台湾军事情况综述]," in National Taiwan Research Committee, ed., *Taiwan 2013* [台湾2013]," Beijing: Jiuzhou Press, 2014.

Bai Guangwei and Ren Guozheng, "An Overview of the Taiwan Military Situation [台湾军事情况综述]," in PLA Academy of Military Science Foreign Military Research Department, ed., *Annual Report on World Military Developments* [世界军事发展年度报告], Beijing: Military Science Press, 2013.

Bellal, Annyssa, ed., *The War Report: Armed Conflict in 2014*, Oxford, UK: Oxford University Press, 2015.

Blasko, Dennis J., *The Chinese Army Today: Tradition and Transformation for the 21st Century*, 2nd edition, New York: Routledge, 2012.

Bremmer, Ian, "5 Statistics That Explained the World This Week," *Politico*, March 2, 2014. As of October 27, 2016:
http://www.politico.com/magazine/story/2014/03/statistics-that-explained-the-world-this-week-104088

Bush, Richard C., *Untying the Knot: Making Peace in the Taiwan Strait*, Washington, D.C.: Brookings Institution Press, 2005.

Cao Zhengrong et al., eds., *Informatized Army Operations* [信息化陆军作战], Beijing: National Defense University Press, 2014.

Central People's Government, People's Republic of China, *The One-China Principle and the Taiwan Issue*, 2000. As of October 27, 2016:
http://www.china.org.cn/english/taiwan/7956.htm

Chase, Michael S., Jeffrey Engstrom, Tai Ming Cheung, Kristen Gunness, Scott Warren Harold, Susan Puska, and Samuel K. Berkowitz, *China's Incomplete Military Transformation: Assessing the Weaknesses of the People's Liberation Army*, Santa Monica, Calif.: RAND Corporation, RR-893-USCC, 2015. As of October 27, 2016:
http://www.rand.org/pubs/research_reports/RR893.html

Chen Kuo-ming and Hwang Lin-chien, "The 29th Hankuang Exercise: Comprehensive Tri-Service Exercise of Important Objectives [漢光29號演習系列: 三軍重要項目總體檢]," *Defence International* [全球防衛雜誌], No. 345, May 2013.

Chen Qing-lin, *National Defense Education: Defense Mobilization* [全民國防教育防衛動員], New Taipei City: New Wun Ching Development Publishing, 2013.

Chung Jung-feng and Christie Chen, "Taiwan Wins Most Gold Medals at Asia Pacific ICT Competition," *Focus Taiwan*, November 26, 2015. As of October 27, 2016:
http://focustaiwan.tw/news/ast/201511260021.aspx

Culpan, Tim, "Apple Opens Secret Laboratory in Taiwan to Develop New Screens," *Bloomberg*, December 14, 2015. As of October 27, 2016:
http://www.bloomberg.com/news/articles/2015-12-15/
apple-said-to-open-secret-lab-in-taiwan-to-develop-displays

"Defence Forces Plans Increase in Refresher Training," *Finland Times*, September 24, 2014. As of October 27, 2016:
http://www.finlandtimes.fi/national/2014/09/24/10379/
Defence-Forces-plans-increase-in-refresher-training

"Defence Minister for Shortening Notice Period," *Finland Times*, November 10, 2015. As of October 27, 2016:
http://www.finlandtimes.fi/national/2015/11/10/22191/
Defence-minister-for-shortening-notice-period

Dong Yuhong and Fan Lihong, "Overview of Taiwan Military Situation in 2008 [2008年台湾军事情况综述]," in National Taiwan Research Committee, ed., *Taiwan 2008* [台湾2008], Beijing: Jiuzhou Press, 2009.

"Don't Expect US Military Aid: General," *Taipei Times*, February 8, 2006.

Easton, Ian, *Able Archers: Taiwan Defense Strategy in an Age of Precision Strike*, Arlington, Va.: Project 2049 Institute, September 2014. As of October 27, 2016:
http://www.project2049.net/documents/
Easton_Able_Archers_Taiwan_Defense_Strategy.pdf

————, *Taiwan's Naval Role in the Rebalance to Asia*, Arlington, Va.: Project 2049 Institute, March 2015. As of October 27, 2016:
http://www.project2049.net/documents/150303_Easton_Taiwans_Naval_Role_in_the_Rebalance.pdf

————, *The Chinese Invasion Threat: Taiwan's Defense and American Strategy in Asia*, Project 2049 Institute, forthcoming.

Elleman, Bruce A., *High Seas Buffer: The Taiwan Patrol Force, 1950–1979*, Newport, R.I.: Naval War College Press, 2012.

"Finland to Contribute in NATO Response Force Readiness," *Finland Times*, November 4, 2014. As of October 27, 2016:
http://www.finlandtimes.fi/national/2014/11/04/11355/Finland--to-contribute-in-NATO-Response-Force-readiness

Finnish Defence Forces, *Annual Report 2011*, 2012.

————, *Annual Report 2012*, 2013.

————, *Annual Report 2014*, 2014.

Friedberg, Aaron, "What Is Strategy?" American Academy of Strategic Education Lecture, Arlington, Va., October 17, 2015.

"Full Text of Anti-Secession Law," *People's Daily*, March 14, 2005. As of October 27, 2016:
http://english.peopledaily.com.cn/200503/14/print20050314_176746.html

Fuller, Liz, and Richard Giragosian, "Georgia: What Is Behind Expansion of Armed Forces?" Radio Free Europe/Radio Liberty, September 19, 2007. As of October 27, 2016:
http://www.rferl.org/content/article/1078720.html

Gao Guangdong et al., "Taiwan Reserve Force Overview [台军后备部队扫描]," *World Outlook* [世界展望], No. 534, February 2006.

"Georgia Lost up to 3,000 Men in S. Ossetia Conflict—Russian Source," *The Financial*, September 14, 2008. As of October 27, 2016:
http://www.finchannel.com/~finchannel/index.php/world/georgia/22195-

Glaser, Bonnie, and Anastasia Mark, "Taiwan's Defense Spending: The Security Consequences of Choosing Butter Over Guns," The Asia Maritime Transparency Initiative and the Center for Strategic and International Studies, March 18, 2015. As of October 27, 2016:
https://amti.csis.org/taiwans-defense-spending-the-security-consequences-of-choosing-butter-over-guns/

Hsieh Chi-peng, "Research on Latest Communist Military Campaign Guidance [共军新時期戰役指導之研究]," *Army Studies Bimonthly* [陸軍學術雙月刊], No. 536, August 2014.

Information Office of the State Council, People's Republic of China, *China's National Defense in 2010*, March 2011. As of October 27, 2016:
http://www.china.org.cn/government/whitepaper/node_7114675.htm

International Institute for Strategic Studies, *The Military Balance 2015*, Vol. 115, No. 1, London, 2015.

Jiang Yanyu, ed., *A Military History of Fifty Years in the Taiwan Area 1949–2006* [台湾地区五十年军事史1949–2006], Beijing: Liberation Army Press, 2013.

Jones, Stephen, *Georgia: A Political History Since Independence*, New York: I.B. Tauris & Co. Ltd., 2013.

Kajimoto, Tetsushi, "GSDF Ready Reservists Sworn In," *The Japan Times*, April 27, 1998. As of October 27, 2016:
http://www.japantimes.co.jp/news/1998/04/27/national/gsdf-ready-reservists-sworn-in/#.VpPGVZMrL1w

Kang Shih-jen, "PLA's Shock and Awe Warfare Is Taiwan's Biggest Threat, Adjustment in Military Planning [Zhonggong zhenshe duitai weixie zui da, guojun niding zuozhan jihua]," Central News Agency [Zhongyangshe], May 5, 2004.

Kaplan, Robert D., "The Geography of Chinese Power," *Foreign Affairs*, May/June 2010. As of October 27, 2016:
http://www.foreignaffairs.com/articles/66205/robert-d-kaplan/the-geography-of-chinese-power

Kapp, Lawrence, and Barbara Salazar Torreon, *Reserve Component Personnel Issues: Questions and Answers*, Washington, D.C.: Congressional Research Service, June 13, 2014. As of October 27, 2016:
https://www.fas.org/sgp/crs/natsec/RL30802.pdf

Khanna, Parag, "National Service for the 21st Century," *The Straits Times*, April 26, 2014. As of October 27, 2016:
http://www.straitstimes.com/opinion/national-service-for-the-21st-century

Kuo Wen-liang, *National Defense Education: Defense Science and Technology* [全民國防教育國防科技], Taipei: NWCD Publishing, 2014.

Lee Hsin-fang, "Military Reservist Numbers Cut, Taiwan's Combat Power to See Gaps by 2020 [後備軍人遞減109年我軍戰力出現缺口]," *Liberty Times* [自由時報], July 30, 2015. As of October 26, 2016:
http://news.ltn.com.tw/news/politics/paper/902328

Liddell Hart, B. H., *Strategy: Second Revised Edition*, New York: Meridian, 1991.

Lim Wee Kiak, "Bringing National Service Up to Date," *The Straits Times*, June 25, 2014. As of October 27, 2016:
http://www.straitstimes.com/opinion/bringing-national-service-up-to-date

Liu Ching-jong, "Research on War Zone Unit Modularization for Homeland Defense [國土防衛中 作戰區部隊模組化之研究]," *Reserve Force Journal* [後備半年刊], April 2011.

———, "Examining the Application of Mechanized Infantry in Future Defense Operations [機步部隊在未來防衛作戰運用之探討]," *Army Studies Bimonthly* [陸軍學術雙月刊], Vol. 49, No. 529, June 2013.

Liu Jian, "Taiwan Military Reserve Force: Difficulties in Becoming Deciding Factor [台军后备部队难成气候]," *Journal of Cross-Strait Relations* [两岸关系], March 2004.

Liu, John, "US, Local Officials Stress ICT at COMPUTEX," *China Times*, June 3, 2015. As of October 27, 2016:
http://www.chinapost.com.tw/taiwan-business/2015/06/03/437500/US-local.htm

Livny, Eric, "On Education and The Sacred Duty of Defending One's Motherland," *The Financial*, November 30, 2015. As of October 27, 2016:
http://www.finchannel.com/index.php/opinion/143-op-ed/52598-on-education-and-the-sacred-duty-of-defending-one-s-motherland

"Local Forces to Be Formed Under Defence Reforms," *Finland Times*, April 29, 2014. As of October 27, 2016:
http://www.finlandtimes.fi/national/2014/04/29/6499/Local-forces-to-be-formed-under-defence-reforms

McCauley, Kevin, "Taiwan Military Reform: Declining Operational Capabilities?" *China Brief*, Vol. 13, No. 12, June 7, 2013.

———, "PLA Special Operations: Combat Missions and Operations Abroad," *China Brief*, Vol. 15, No. 17, September 3, 2015. As of October 27, 2016:
https://jamestown.org/program/pla-special-operations-combat-missions-and-operations-abroad/

Mei, Fu S., "Operational Changes in Taiwan's Han Kuang Military Exercises 2008–2010," *China Brief*, Vol. 10, No. 11, May 27, 2010. As of October 27, 2016:
https://jamestown.org/program/operational-changes-in-taiwans-han-kuang-military-exercises-2008-2010/

Menabde, Giorgi, "Georgia Reviews Results of Its Military Reforms," *Eurasia Daily Monitor*, Vol. 11, No. 21, February 4, 2014. As of October 27, 2016:
https://jamestown.org/program/georgia-reviews-results-of-its-military-reform/

Ministry of Defence of Georgia, *National Military Strategy*, 2014a. As of October 27, 2016:
http://www.mod.gov.ge/assets/up-modul/uploads/pdf/NMS-ENG.pdf

———, *White Book 2014*, 2014b. As of October 27, 2016:
http://www.mod.gov.ge/assets/up-modul/uploads/pdf/WB_2014_ENG.pdf

Ministry of Defence of Singapore, "Factsheet—Reservist on Voluntary Extended Reserve Service (ROVERS) Scheme," last updated on May 12, 2005. As of October 27, 2016:
http://www.mindef.gov.sg/imindef/press_room/official_releases/nr/1998/aug/20aug98_nr/20aug98_fs2.print.img.html

———, "Fact Sheet: Committee to Strengthen National Service," May 8, 2013. As of October 27, 2016:
http://www.mindef.gov.sg/imindef/press_room/official_releases/nr/2013/may/08may13_nr.html#.VpPW9JMrL1w

———, "Strengthening NS: The Committee," web page, 2014a. As of October 27, 2016:
http://www.mindef.gov.sg/strengthenNS/the-committee.html

———, "Strengthen National Service," web page, last updated on May 22, 2014b. As of October 27, 2016:
http://www.mindef.gov.sg/imindef/key_topics/strengthen_ns.html

———, "Recommendations by the Committee to Strengthen National Service," news release, last updated on June 10, 2014c. As of October 27, 2016:
http://www.mindef.gov.sg/imindef/press_room/official_releases/nr/2014/jun/10jun14_nr/10jun14_fs.html#.VpPW65MrL1w

———, "NS Matters: For NSmen," web page, last updated on October 29, 2014d. As of October 27, 2016:
http://www.mindef.gov.sg/imindef/mindef_websites/topics/nsmatters/nsmen/roles_as_nsmen.html#.VpVnUZMrL1w

———, "NS Matters: About Us," web page, last updated on January 15, 2016. As of October 27, 2016:
http://www.mindef.gov.sg/imindef/mindef_websites/topics/nsmatters/about_us.html#.VpAZ0pMrL1w

Ministry of Defense of Japan, *Defense of Japan 2005*, "Chapter 5: People and the Defense Agency/SDF," 2005. As of October 27, 2016:
http://www.mod.go.jp/e/publ/w_paper/pdf/2005/5.pdf

———, *Defense of Japan 2006*, "Defense Chronology," 2006. As of October 27, 2016:
http://www.mod.go.jp/e/publ/w_paper/pdf/2006/8-1-1.pdf

———, *Defense of Japan 2007*, "Chapter 4: Citizens of Japan, the Ministry of Defense and the SDF," 2007. As of October 27, 2016:
http://www.mod.go.jp/e/publ/w_paper/pdf/2007/40Part3_Chap4_Sec1.pdf

———, *Defense of Japan 2015*, 2015a.

———, "Defense Programs and Budget of Japan: Overview of FY2016 Budget Request," August 2015b. As of October 27, 2016:
http://www.mod.go.jp/e/d_budget/pdf/271016.pdf

Ministry of Foreign Affairs of Georgia, *National Security Concept of Georgia*, no date. As of October 27, 2016:
http://www.mfa.gov.ge/MainNav/ForeignPolicy/NationalSecurityConcept.aspx?lang=en-US

Ministry of National Defense of the Republic of China, "About Reserve Command: Missions," web page, no date-a. As of September 24, 2015:
http://afrc.mnd.gov.tw/PeopleAmry/AboutAFRC/net_2-1-1.html

———, "About Reserve Command," web page, no date-b. As of September 17, 2015:
http://afrc.mnd.gov.tw/PeopleAmry/AboutAFRC/net_2-2-1.html

———, *2013 Quadrennial Defense Review*, March 2013. As of October 27, 2016:
http://qdr.mnd.gov.tw/encontent.html

———, *Republic of China National Defense Report 2015*
[中華民國104年國防報告書], October 2015. As of October 27, 2016:
http://report.mnd.gov.tw/

"MND Estimates China's Future Military Stance," *China Post*, February 8, 2006.

"MND Mobilizes Reservists for Tung Hsin Exercise," *China Post,* August 22, 2016.

Office of Naval Intelligence, *The PLA Navy: New Capabilities and Missions for the 21st Century*, Washington, D.C., 2015.

O'Hanlon, Michael, "Why China Cannot Conquer Taiwan," *International Security*, Vol. 25, No. 2, Fall 2000, pp. 51–86.

Olsen, Edward A., *U.S.-Japan Strategic Reciprocity: A Neo-Internationalist View*, 1985.

Ong Hwee Hwee, "Budget Backgrounder: National Service," *The Straits Times*, March 6, 2014. As of October 27, 2016:
http://www.straitstimes.com/singapore/budget-backgrounder-national-service

O'Rourke, Ronald, *China Naval Modernization: Implications for U.S. Navy Capabilities*, Washington, D.C.: Congressional Research Service Report, July 28, 2015.

Pan Shaoying and Zhang Yingzhen, eds., *Research on Foreign (and Taiwan) Army and Military Training* [外(台)军陆军军事训练研究], Beijing: Liberation Army Press, 2006.

"Penghu Wude Joint Counter Amphibious Exercise
[澎湖五德聯信聯合反登陸操演]," *Defence International* [全球防衛雜誌], May 2013.

"Republic of Georgia, Background Brief: CENEX 2013," University of Denver Josef Korbel School of International Studies, Crisis Engagement and Negotiation Exercise (CENEX) 2013. As of October 27, 2016:
https://www.du.edu/korbel/cenex/media/documents/cenex2013/cenex2013_georgia_background.pdf

"Reserve Mobilization: Counterattack after Tamsui Raid and Taipei Port Attack [後備動員淡水反突擊台北港反擊]," *Defence International* [全球防衛雜誌], No. 362, October 2014.

Rosen, Stephen, "What Is Strategy?" American Academy of Strategic Education Lecture, Arlington, Va., October 17, 2015.

"SDF Struggling to Attract Enough Reservists," *The Japan Times*, August 19, 2014. As of October 27, 2016:
http://www.japantimes.co.jp/news/2014/08/19/national/sdf-struggling-to-attract-enough-reservists/#.Vo_UKpMrL1w

"Send in the Reserves," *Armed Forces Journal*, February 1, 2012. As of October 27, 2016:
http://www.armedforcesjournal.com/send-in-the-reserves/

Shou Xiaosong, ed., *Science of Military Strategy* [战略学], Beijing: Military Science Press, 2013.

Squires, Nick, "Finland Tells 900,000 Reservists Their Roles 'In the Event of War,'" *The Telegraph*, May 21, 2015. As of October 27, 2016:
http://www.telegraph.co.uk/news/worldnews/europe/finland/11621512/Finland-tells-900000-reservists-their-roles-in-the-event-of-war.html

Stokes, Mark A., *Revolutionizing Taiwan's Security: Leveraging C4ISR for Traditional and Nontraditional Challenges*, Arlington, Va.: Project 2049 Institute, September 2009. As of October 27, 2016:
https://project2049.net/documents/revolutionizing_taiwans_security_leveraging_c4isr_for_traditional_and_non_traditional_challenges.pdf

Stokes, Mark A., and Russell Hsiao, *The People's Liberation Army General Political Department: Political Warfare with Chinese Characteristics*, Arlington, Va.: Project 2049 Institute, October 2013. As of October 26, 2016:
http://www.project2049.net/documents/PLA_General_Political_Department_Liaison_Stokes_Hsiao.pdf

Stokes, Mark A., and Tiffany Ma, *Taiwan, the People's Liberation Army, and the Struggle with Nature*, Arlington, Va.: Project 2049 Institute, May 2011. As of October 27, 2016:
http://project2049.net/documents/taiwan_morakot_natural_hazards_peoples_liberation_army_stokes_ma.pdf

"Taiwan Population 2015," *World Population Review*, September 13, 2015. As of October 27, 2016:
http://worldpopulationreview.com/countries/taiwan-population/

"Taiwan to Spend $2.5 Billion on Anti-Missile Systems," *Defense News*, August 30, 2014.

Tatsumi, Yuki, *Great Eastern Japan Earthquake: "Lessons Learned" for Japanese Defense Policy*, Stimson Center, November 2012. As of October 27, 2016:
http://www.stimson.org/content/
great-eastern-japan-earthquake-lessons-learned-japanese-defense-policy

Tsai Ho-hsun, "Research on the Communist Military's Division Landing Operations [共軍師登陸作戰之研究]," *Army Studies Bimonthly* [陸軍學術雙月刊], Vol. 50, No. 537, October 2014.

Tseng Wei-chen and Chen Wei-han, ""Unification Support Dives: Poll," *Taipei Times*, July 26, 2015. As of October 27, 2016:
http://www.taipeitimes.com/News/taiwan/archives/2015/07/26/2003623930

U.S. Census Bureau, "U.S. and World Population Clock," 2016. As of September 25, 2015:
http://www.census.gov/popclock/

U.S. Department of Defense, *Report to Congress on Implementation of the Taiwan Relations Act*, Washington, D.C., 1999.

———, *Annual Report to Congress: Military and Security Developments Involving the People's Republic of China 2015*, 2015. As of October 27, 2016:
http://www.defense.gov/Portals/1/Documents/pubs/2015_China_Military_Power_Report.pdf

Wachman, Alan, *Why Taiwan? Geostrategic Rationales for China's Territorial Integrity*, Stanford, Calif.: Stanford University Press, 2007.

Wang Weixing, "Taiwan Military [台湾军事]," in Ning Sao, ed., *2006–2008 Research Report on Taiwan Strait Situation* [2006–2008年台海局势研究报告], Beijing: Jiuzhou Press, 2006.

Wang, Yuan-kang, "Taiwan Public Opinion on Cross-Strait Security Issues: Implications for US Foreign Policy," *Strategic Studies Quarterly*, Summer 2013. As of October 27, 2016:
http://homepages.wmich.edu/~ymz8097/articles/wang_taiwan%20public%20opinion.pdf

Wilborn, Thomas L., *Japan's Self-Defense Forces: What Dangers to Northeast Asia?* Strategic Studies Institute, U.S. Army War College, May 1, 1994.

Wong, Edward, Jane Perlez, and Chris Buckley, "China Announces Cuts of 300,000 Troops at Military Parade Showing Its Might," *New York Times*, September 2, 2015. As of October 27, 2016:
http://www.nytimes.com/2015/09/03/world/asia/beijing-turns-into-ghost-town-as-it-gears-up-for-military-parade.html?_r=0

"A Working Conference of National Reserve Forces Committee," *Newsday Georgia*, October 23, 2015. As of October 27, 2016:
http://newsday.ge/new/index.php/en/component/k2/
item/9301-a-working-conference-of-national-reserve-forces-committee

Xu Zhong, "Analyzing Taiwan Military Reserve Force Building
[析台军后备力量建设]," *China Militia* [中国民兵], No. 2, 2007.

Yang You-hung, "Research into Communist Military's Joint Island Landing
Offensive Campaign Capabilities [共軍聯合島嶼進攻戰役能力研究]," *Reserve Force Journal* [後備半年刊], No. 88, October 2013.

Yeh Chien-chung and Chen Hong-diao, "Evaluating Infantry Unit Urban
Warfare Training [步兵部隊城鎮作戰訓練之探討]," *Army Studies Bimonthly*
[陸軍學術雙月刊], No. 537, October 2014.

Yeh, Joseph, "Defense Ministry Amends Reservist Call-Up Loophole," *China Post*,
April 22, 2016.

You Tai-lang, "Han Kuang Exercise: Back-Up Runway Landings Successful
[漢光演習 副跑道降落圓滿達成]," *Liberty Times* [自由時報], April 18, 2012. As
of October 27, 2016:
http://news.ltn.com.tw/news/local/paper/576866

Zhou Yi et al., "Assessing Taiwan's Ballistic Missile and Cruise Missile
Development [台湾弹道导弹与巡航导弹发展评析]," *Winged Missile Journal*
[飞航导弹], No. 5, 2005.

Zhu Feng, "Why Taiwan Really Matters to China," *China Brief*, Vol. 4, No. 19,
September 30, 2004. As of October 27, 2016:
https://jamestown.org/program/why-taiwan-really-matters-to-china/